THE CHILDREN OF THE MACHINE

THE CHILDREN OF THE MACHINE

Alan Dent

First published March 2025

© Alan Dent

ISBN 978-1-913144-70-8

PENNILESS PRESS PUBLICATIONS

Website : www.pennilesspress.co.uk/books

X received an e-mail inviting him for an interview though he had applied for no job. It was fortunate as he'd been out of work for three months since his supervisor found he had an affection for his secretary. In truth, it was more her affection for him. She suggested they might go to the café in the park at lunchtime and as he'd walked past it many times but never been in, he accepted. It was a pretty little place and with the river running nearby and the trees swaying in the breeze, the tension which kept him working gave way and he could have stayed all afternoon. While he was gazing out of the window, she shook her hair free. When he looked at her it was loose and cascading while in the office she kept it neatly brushed and tied. She had thick, auburn hair which attracted him because it reminded him of his mother and sister. Her blue eyes were fixing him. He was tempted to lay his hand on her knee but thought he might be misinterpreting. When they left and he was behind her he put his palms gently on her shoulders and she gave a little skip and a laugh. They arrived back five minutes late which brought the warning letter mentioning the two occasions he'd been late in the morning.

"It's only twice in four years," he said to the supervisor, "and both times the train was cancelled."

"Get an earlier train."

"But I don't know if it's cancelled until I arrive at the station."

"Then arrive at station early."

Though he was on time subsequently, the formal warning was issued.

"It's not just your time-keeping."

"What is it?"

"I've got all evidence I need," said the supervisor, pulling a file from his desk drawer.

1

"Can I see it?"

"Of course not."

"Why not?"

"It's for management."

He asked the union rep what to do and was told it might be best to take a compromise deal.

"But I don't want to lose my job," he said.

"No, but it's the lesser of the evils."

He was given a month's notice for misconduct. Since finishing he'd lived by selling records from the collection he inherited from his father. He'd applied for benefits but had to prove he was seeking employment during the whole of the working week.

"It's absurd," he said to the employee, "I'm not qualified for any of these jobs."

"What are you qualified for?"

"Office work."

"This is an office job."

"Yes, but I have no accounting skills."

"Perhaps you should get some."

His father had amassed hundreds of jazz records many of them with sleeves signed by the musicians. At first, he sold them to dealers but realised he could get a much better price by finding the collector who wanted them so began to advertise. A copy of *Someday My Prince Will Come* signed by John Coltrane brought three thousand, which kept him for two months. He rang the given number.

"I've had a message calling me for interview. I'm a bit puzzled as I don't recall applying."

"You wouldn't be called if you weren't required."

"Do I need to bring anything with me?"

"What would you like to bring?"

"My certificates."

"What use are they?"

"I thought you might like to see them."

"If we wanted to see them we would ask."

The building was on an estate well out of town, a place he'd never been. The bus took him within a mile, the remainder he walked.

"What's your registration number?" the receptionist asked.

"I came by bus."

"But the bus doesn't come this way."

"No, I got off at the turning circle and walked."

"You walked?"

"Yes."

"Then I can't fill in your registration number."

"I don't have a car."

"Is it in for repairs?"

"No, I don't possess one."

"Did you have an accident?"

"No, I've never owned one."

"That's most unusual. I'll put it's in for repairs."

X noticed the receptionist's lips which had obviously been treated with filler. Her eyebrows were thick black lines. Her face was artificially tanned and her nails were long, each bearing a unique decoration. He thought of the secretary who was the source of his current malaise and how she permitted herself to be natural and it occurred to him he'd heard nothing of her since his departure.

"I'll show you into the waiting-room but please don't talk to the other candidates."

He was conducted to an empty room, very comfortably appointed. He settled himself in the corner of one of the two dark blue velvet sofas. Pop music was piped through speakers high in the corners, though he neither recognised nor liked it. On the table before him were four piles of magazines. He took the top one from the first pile, studied its cover and set it to the left, continuing in the same way. There were publications about travel, gardening, fitness, DIY, interior design, decorating, baking, cooking, entertaining, aviation, trains, cars, royalty, celebrities, vegetarianism, running, cycling, mountain climbing, sailing, hair styles, body decoration, wine, coffee, beer, property, horoscopes, television, pop music, bird watching. He made the piles neat and sat back once more. He must have fallen asleep because when he woke the room was quite dark. He reached into his pocket for his phone but it wasn't there. He tried to recall the exact layout so he could make his way to the light switch which he assumed must be by the door. Wasn't there a window behind him? He could open the curtains or the blind and let in some light from the street lamps; but when he felt the wall it was flat. "I'm sure there was a window," he said to himself. He stretched out his arms in the way typical of a blind person and moving to the right his fingertips hit the cold surface. "Ah, now if I simply follow this to the corner I should find the switch." Edging slowly in case there was some piece of furniture he'd forgotten about he shuffled till his fingers sensed the corner but running his palms over the wall discovered nothing. Moving to his left he found the door. Was there a lock which would let him out? He gripped the metal handle, tugged it down two or three times and pulled. There was nothing for it but to raise the alarm. He began to hammer with his knuckles and to shout: "Hey! I'm locked in here. Can you hear me? Let me out it's pitch dark." At length he resigned and decided to sit down. There was a second sofa. Where was it? Perhaps if he crossed the room he'd find it but it was safer as he could see nothing to retrace his steps. Seated once more he at least had the safety of knowing where he was. There'd been some mistake. When the night was over he'd be released and would be able to make a complaint. He stretched himself full length and closed his eyes reflecting that he hadn't been interviewed. What kind of incompetent organisation was this? Well, not under any circumstances would he work for them.

He must have nodded off again, in spite of his anxiety. When he woke, light was filtering through the curtains behind him. He pulled them wide open. It was clearly early morning. "Someone must be around now," he thought, went to the door and began hammering and shouting again. At once he heard his ringtone, went to the table where his phone was by one of the piles of magazines.

"Hello?"

"What's the problem?"

"The problem? I've been in here all night. The door is locked."

"Locked?"

"Yes, could you let me out now, please?"

He felt he'd put sufficient sternness and displeasure into his tone.

"The door's open."

He yanked on the handle and let himself out. Reception, he recalled was to his left. He pushed through the double glass doors. The receptionist was at her desk.

"I've been here all night. I was locked in."

"Do you want some breakfast?"

"Breakfast?"

"Yes, and to freshen up. A bath or a shower."

"What I'd like to know is why I was imprisoned here overnight."

"You were free to go after the interview."

"I didn't have an interview."

"Then you must be first on the list for this morning."

She checked her screen.

"Yes, you are. But you've time to have a shower and some breakfast. We can provide whatever you like."

"Will I be interviewed by the boss?"

"The boss? Who do you mean?"

"The person who runs this organisation."

"Ms D? Yes, she's doing the interviews this morning."

"Good, then I'll be able to tell her what I think of her outfit."

"What would you like first, breakfast or a shower?"

"I think I'd like a shower first, and I need a shave but I've nothing with me."

"I can see to that. Wet or electric?"

"Electric."

"I can offer you a comfortable wet shave."

"Who will do that?"

"Me."

"But you're the receptionist."

"I have many skills."

She led him to a lift which rose to the seventh floor.

"I didn't realise the building was so tall."

"You can't see the tower from the road."

The doors opened onto a broad open area, carpeted in deep red and furnished with armchairs, sofas and low tables.

6

There were plants and white, blue, red and yellow flowers around the periphery and gentle music piping. The tall windows permitted a view of the hills to the east and the suburbs of the town to the west. He followed her across the centre of the space and into a bathroom.

"There are bathrobes in the cupboard. If you leave your clothes in the basket, I'll have them laundered. I'll be back in a minute."

X wondered if he should leave. It would be easy enough to get back to the lift, down to reception and through the front door. He tried the handle but couldn't get out. "This is preposterous," he thought. All the same, he took off his clothes, put them in the basket she'd pointed out and slipped on a white bathrobe. It was clean, fresh and very comfortable. "Well, they're looking after me," he reflected. "Might as well make the best of it. Once the interview's over, I can go on my way." The receptionist retuned dressed in a short, white tunic cut low so her cleavage was visible.

"Well, sit yourself here," she said, standing behind a black leather chair before a wash-basin and mirror, " and we'll make a start."

He sat down and looked at himself in the mirror. His stubble had grown overnight and his face was pasty, but otherwise he looked quite normal. He was almost impelled to blurt, "Ah, that's me." The receptionist tilted the chair back, rubbed a shaving brush vigorously against the soap and began to apply the lather.

"I asked for electric," he said.

"Yes, but I think you'll enjoy this and it gives a closer finish."

Though he considered her behaviour intrusive he reasoned it was only a shave, she seemed expert and perhaps he would appreciate it. As she leaned, her breasts pushed against his upper arm. At a certain point, she straddled his legs, the better to pass the cut-throat over his chin. Her inner thighs were against his. She lowered herself to attend to his neck and her breasts touched his chest. When the hot towels were on his face she said:

"I assume you'll want the assisted shower."

"No, I'm quite capable of showering myself."

"I know that, but as its part of the service, why should you turn it down?"

"I thought I was here to be interviewed."

"Of course, but if you're going to belong to the organisation, we want you to be happy here."

She pulled aside the curtain of the shower cubicle and set the water running.

"They're power-showers," she said. "The best you can get. Do you like the water hot?"

"Not too hot."

"Come along." He stood before the cubicle.

"Well, in you go," she said.

He let the bathrobe fall to floor and stepped in quickly so she could see him only from behind but at once she was next to him, her breasts against his back.

"Shall I shampoo your hair first?"

"I can do it myself."

"You'll find I do a better job. I'll massage your scalp .It's very good for the circulation. Turn and face me."

He did as she asked in spite of his embarrassment.

"That's good" she said. "You have a healthy response." When the shower was over she disappeared to return with a pile of freshly laundered clothes very similar to his own.

"These aren't mine."

"No, yours have gone to the laundry. They'll be ready tomorrow."

The cleanliness from having showered, physical satisfaction and the pleasant feel of the clean clothes almost overcame his unease as he followed to a pair of dark blue double doors which she pulled open and passed through. The dining-room was wide and long with tall windows which admitted a glorious light. There were thirty or so round tables draped with white cloths whose points almost touched the carpet which was the same colour as the double doors. Each table was laid for breakfast: silver cutlery, dark blue napkins, silver condiments and toast racks. In the middle was an island laden with fruit, cereals, yogurt, cheeses, pastries, cooked meats, jugs of orange and grapefruit juice.

"Choose a table," she said. "I recommend one by the windows on the right, the views are stunning. Help yourself to whatever you like from the island. A waitress will take your order for cooked breakfast."

He approached the island with caution as the receptionist pushed through the doors at the opposite end. Normally, he didn't eat much at the start of the day: dry oats with natural yogurt on the advice of his doctor who had told him it was good for keeping cholesterol low and a cup of black tea. With an empty white bowl in his hand he wondered again if he should make his escape. There was no one around. Yet it seemed churlish to turn down such an offer. From the tall jar of oats he poured a healthy pile, topped it with a spoonful of summer fruits over which he dropped several blobs of yogurt. Without thinking, he went to a table on the right and looked out at the hills where he'd walked many times. When the interview was over he might go home and slip on his boots. He was in the mood for pushing up a thousand feet and standing alone in the fresh air. The first mouthful stirred his appetite. The consistency of the yogurt and the cold sweetness of the fruit together with the dryness of the oats was a lovely combination. From the far doors, a young waitress appeared dressed in a short black skirt, a white blouse and black tights.

"Good morning, sir. Did you sleep well?"

He looked up wondering how she knew he'd spent the night there.

"Not really," he said. "I wasn't intending to stay. I just came for an interview, you see."

"Yes, all our guests do, sir. Cooked breakfast?"

"What's available."

"There's the menu, sir," she said, picking it up from behind the toast rack and handing it to him. He noticed porridge was on offer and wished he'd known.

"I don't suppose I can have some porridge?"

"You can have what you like, sir," she said with a certain intonation.

"Well, I'll have some porridge. A small portion. Or at least not too big. And the full English but without baked beans."

"How would you like your eggs?"

"Scrambled."

"How many?"

"Three."

"Toast?"

"Yes, please, brown."

"Tea or coffee?"

" Tea, decaffeinated, please"

"No problem," and she lifted the toast rack and minced away. The tea arrived first, then the toast and as soon as his bowl was empty, the porridge, steaming. When she came to take away his empty dish and he asked for some butter, she giggled and said,

"Oh, how silly of me."

The wholesome food filled and fortified him. He requested a second rack of toast and pot of tea. How long had he been there? The receptionist hadn't shown her face. He was alone. Why were there thirty tables and only one guest. Guest? He wasn't a guest. He resolved to make a hash of the interview. They would see he wasn't right for the place and off he'd go, but his breakfast finished and the table cleared, no one came to see him. He tried his mobile to check the time but it didn't respond. It was in need of charging but usually it would still display the hour. Well, if they chose to leave him alone, why shouldn't he walk out? It was impolite of them. Did they think he had nothing better to do? He screwed up the napkin which had been on his knees, pushed back his chair and headed for the doors. Going down in the lift he wondered if the receptionist would be back in her place and if she would try to stop him. Too bad. He would thank her for the breakfast, say nothing about the rest, and leave; but when he came out of the lift on the ground floor, a man in a commissioner's uniform greeted him.

"Are you ready for the interview now, sir?"

"Not at all," he said. "I've no idea what time it is. No one has told me what time the interview is. I'm not in the mood to be interviewed now."

"Perhaps you'd like a little rest, sir?"

"A rest?"

"Yes, after a good meal a nap is often pleasant. I can show you to your room."

"My room?"

"We allocate all our clients a room, sir. Most comfortable. Bed, television, en suite. Shall we?"

"But I'm not a client."

"In a manner of speaking no, in a manner of speaking yes."

"I've changed my mind about this job. I'm going to leave now."

"I'm afraid all the exits are locked."

"Now, just a minute. You can't keep me here against my will."

"Quite right, sir. You came of your own free will and will leave in the same way, once the doors are unlocked."

"But why are they locked?"

"Security, sir. You have to take that for granted."

"Security from what? I'm not any kind of threat."

"You may well not be, but how can the organization know that? If we treat everyone as a threat we're sure not to miss anyone."

At that moment, the receptionist appeared. She was brisk and cheery. Her smile made him feel she was a friend.

"Would you like to follow me?" she said, at which the commissioner turned and left. X did as she asked.

"As a matter of fact," he said to her back, "I'm ready to leave now. I no longer want to go ahead with the interview."

"Everybody feels like that at some point of the process," she said.

He followed because there was nothing else he could do. She led him to what appeared to be a hotel. Behind an attractive, curved, wooden feature a young woman whose hair was brushed back apart from two wisps which fell at either side of her face, greeted them. Her smile was gracious and welcoming. "Give me the key for 307, said his guide and when it was handed over they stepped into the lift in the corner which smelled of lilacs and carried them smoothly to the third floor.

The key was a card the receptionist waved before the door handle where a green light showed and they entered. It was more of a suite than a room, which troubled him.

"Am I going to be here some time?" he wondered.

She slipped the card into the slot on the wall and turned on the lights.

"This is the bathroom. You won't be wanting another shower just yet will you?"

"No."

There was a bath, a wash basin, a full-length mirror. The tiles were black and white, set in a pattern he quickly tried to fathom.

"The floor can be slippy when it's wet," she said. "But I can always be here to give you a hand."

The bed was big enough for four and opposite was a dark blue sofa. Above it, as above the bedhead was a huge, flat screen tv. His guide opened the fridge in the corner.

"There's plenty to drink," she said. "Would you like a glass of champagne."

"Not now."

"You'll be comfortable here."

"Actually, I've made up my mind to leave."

"Is the room not to your taste?"

"It's fine, but I no longer wish to be considered for the appointment."

"But you are considered."

"I know, but I no longer wish to be. I withdraw."

"I'm afraid that's not within our protocols."

"Maybe not, but I didn't sign up to them."

"Everyone is signed up to them, as you put it."

"I can't be expected to follow protocols I haven't agreed to."

"We all must, what would happen to society otherwise?"

"I don't know. It's not my business. I simply want to go home.

"But if you go home you are putting the whole of society at risk. The well-being and happiness of all rest on the protocols being followed to the letter."

"I don't know what they are."

"Why do you need to? Imagine if all the people had to know the protocols. Wouldn't that waste a lot of time and effort? If the leaders know what they are, the rest of us do as we're told and everyone's happiness is protected."

"But I'm not happy to stay here."

"Then have some champagne and a bath. I'll give you a complete body wash and you'll feel fine.

"I don't like champagne."

"There are plenty of other drinks. Vodka. Whiskey. Beer. Or drugs if you prefer."

"What drugs?"

"Whatever you choose."

"Isn't that against the law?"

"The law doesn't apply here. We have special dispensations. The leaders can't be expected to comply with the restrictions which apply to the people. That wouldn't be fair."

X moved to the window, pulled aside the net and looked out over flat roofs, a little courtyard where a man in unform was patrolling, trees beyond which suggested countryside.

"I wouldn't mind going for a walk," he said.

"You don't want to tire yourself before your interview."

"When is the interview?"

"When the leaders are ready for you."

"I could be an old man by then," he said.

She cast a hard, sidelong glance at him.

"But you'll be well looked-after in the meantime."

"I prefer to look after myself."

She sat on the sofa, unbuttoned her blouse, took off her bra, slipped her skirt to the floor and removed her thong.

"Now," she said, opening her legs and beginning to rub herself, "come and pleasure me. Come on. I need it. Come on."

He turned away from her and looked out of the window.

"Would you prefer me to pleasure you?"

"I'd prefer you to leave," he said.

"I'll be back when you're in a better mood."

X lay on the bed alone. It couldn't be too difficult to make his escape. From the window he could surely clamber onto one of those roofs. There was the man below, but he could watch for him. He could find his way to a fire escape. There was sure to be one. Once on the ground, he'd make his way to the entrance. He went to the window. The uniformed man was still pacing. The opening light in the corner was restricted in its movement. He inspected it. Two screws. He needed a screwdriver. Perhaps a knife would do. He called reception. "I'd like something to eat. Toast and pate, please." He took the plate from the waitress, put it on the bedside table and inspected the knife. Its rounded end fit into the groove but when he tried to turn, the stiffness made it jump out. He needed to press hard but he wasn't a strong man, nor adept with tools. The idea came to him of ringing his neighbour who was intensely practical but he remembered his mobile was blocked. No, he had to persevere. He slipped the end in once more pushed hard and twisted with all the petty force of his thin forearm. The pacing man looked up. For thirty seconds he stared before gently shaking his head. X withdrew the knife and went back to the bed. He could wait till dark. It might be perilous to try to scramble onto the roof without light. If he fell, it would be the end of him, but what was so bad about that? Better to die in the attempt than be imprisoned for the rest of his life.

A sudden surge in his chest made him leap from the bed. For the rest of his life? Imprisoned?

He tried the door, went to the telephone.

"I seem to be locked in my room."

"Yes, sir, that's for your security."

"I'd like to stretch my legs. Can you open the door, please?"

"Food is on its way up, sir. If you'd like a session in the gym after you've eaten I can book you in."

"No, I don't like gyms, I like to walk in the open air."

"The gym is very good for your health, sir."

"I dare say, but it's not what I choose. If you can open the door I can sort myself out as far as my fitness goes."

"I'm afraid we can't have people wandering the site unsupervised. It would put us all at risk."

"In any case, I've pointed out I no longer want to go through with the interview."

"The interview can't be cancelled, sir. It would throw our plans into chaos."

Food was on the way up. Perhaps that would provide the opportunity to force his way out. If it was brought by a waitress, he would probably be stronger, though not necessarily. Many women were physically more robust. It was worth a try. He blenched from the idea of attacking her. A punch in the face or a kick in the shins. No. The thought of inflicting pain made him wince. Even the man below in uniform, a nasty presence, he couldn't have struck. It wasn't merely cowardice, knowing the guard, if that's what he was, would be stronger and probably trained in self-defence. Had he been armed: a club, a knife, a gun, he wouldn't have wanted to hurt him. Yet if he pushed past the waitress, if a waitress it was, he might do no more than unbalance her, send the tray of food flying. That wouldn't be beyond him. He could rush along the corridor, down the stairs and out of the front entrance. Could he remember the way? Would there be locked doors? How was it a place so easy to enter was so hard to leave? He lay on the bed. There was nothing to occupy his attention but the television; when he tried to access the news, he found there was nothing but programmes about the institution, the site, the leaders. This was very odd. He called reception.

"There seems to be something wrong with the television in my room."

"Isn't it working, sir?"

"Yes, but I can't access the news."

"That's our policy. The news is too stressful. It might impair your interview performance."

"I'm quite capable of dealing with the news."

"Yes, you may think so, but the leaders know better."

"Can you tell the leaders…no, I'll tell them myself."

"If you'd like some entertainment I can have that streamed for you."

"What kind of entertainment?"

"Whatever you prefer, sir."

"Well, if it's better than what's on now, I'll try it."

"Fine, sir, switch to channel 100."

While he was waiting for the programme to appear, the knock came. But how could he open the door.

"I'm locked in," he called, standing a few inches back.

"Try the handle."

It was a man's voice. Would he be able to shove past him. Perhaps he would be big and muscular. If only he wasn't himself a slight, unimposing figure. Still, it was worth a try. He had the element of surprise. He tried the handle. The door opened. There was a boy of seventeen, tall but skinny with a tray. X slipped his palms beneath and pushed upwards. The chicken leg, potatoes, gravy, carrots, parsnips, cauliflower cheese, broccoli and broad beans, the teapot and its contents, the milk jug likewise were distributed across the carpet. X pelted to the corridor's end. The double doors were locked. He looked back. The boy was on his hands and knees picking up the wasted food in his fingers, scraping with the side of his hand at the cauliflower cheese.

"Open this door,"called X.

The boy raised his face. His expression was impassive. He looked down at his messy little task.

"Hey," called X, "open up. I have to leave."

The boy raised his head once more and shook it gently. He was just a boy after all. He had to do what he was told. Of course he did. X walked back to him.

"Sorry about that. I didn't mean to make work."

The boy looked up briefly.

"Look, if you can let me out, I'll make it worth your while. Just let me slip through the door when you leave."

"I didn't come through the door."

X looked along the corridor. There were three doors on each side, presumably leading to rooms like his own.

"How did you get here?"

"The lift."

"Where's the lift?"

"There."

The boy pointed with his hand coated in cooled melted cheese to the next door on the right. X went to open it. Before him was an unprotected lift shaft. Looking down he could see the top of the compartment.

"How do I call it?" he asked.

"You can't."

"What's the use of a lift you can't summon?"

"It's controlled from the centre."

"What centre?"

The boy shrugged.

"I don't know. That's what people say. The centre. That's where everything is controlled from."

"Well, how will you get down?"

"They'll tell me when the lift is arriving."

"How?"

The boy pointed to his ear. X moved closer and inspected.

"Okay. When they tell you, we'll get in the lift together."

The food was back on the plate, the teapot on the tray. The boy took a cloth from his pocket and began to rub at the wet stains.

"You need to get cleaned up," said X. "Come into my room."

The boy complied. In the bathroom he ran his hands under the water. As he was using the towel he put his right index to his ear.

"The lift?" said X.

"Someone's coming up with a new tray of food."

"I don't want food."

"They have to feed you well. They'll be in trouble if you're malnourished."

"Trouble with who?"

"I don't know, the centre."

"Listen, before they get here, let me show you something." He took the boy to the window.

"You see those two screws. If I can get them out, I can clamber onto the roof. I need a screwdriver."

The boy drew down the corners of his mouth in a non-committal expression.

"If you can get me one."

The boy shook his head.

"I'm food. I don't get near tools."

"But don't you have a screwdriver at home?"

"This is my home."

"Can't you talk to someone?"

"I don't know."

"Find out. Make an excuse to come up here. We could escape together."

"I don't want to escape."

"How long have you been here?"

"I was born here."

"Are your parents here."

"I don't know."

"You don't know your parents."

"I've always been looked after

"Are you happy?"

"I don't know."

"It's a small request. A screwdriver. There must be one somewhere in this complex."

"I'm sure there are many, but I don't see them. I have my allotted routes and duties. If I diverge, they'll notice."

"Who?"

"The leaders, or their assistants."

"I was brought here for an interview, you see, but I have no interest in a job here anymore. They seem to think they're doing me a favour by keeping me here, but I need to get back to my life."

"There's nothing I can do," said the boy.

X wondered if he should try to overpower him. He was a few inches shorter and not heavily-built. Maybe he could force him. Yet even if he did twist his arm up his back and make him agree, how were they going to get out together? And once the boy was gone, what guarantee was there he'd return. No, it was more sensible to be his friend.

"Listen," said X, "I don't know anyone here. Maybe we could spend a bit of time together."

"What for?"

"To get to know one another."

"Why?"

"Well, I think we might get on well together."

"I have no time. When I'm not working I have to sleep or catch up with the messages."

"What messages?"

"From the leaders."

The sound of the lift doors opening made the boy head for the exit. In a moment, a young woman was in the room with a tray.

"I believe there was an accident," she said. "Here's your meal."

"No," said X, "not an accident. I deliberately upset the tray. I was trying to escape."

"The excitement must have made you hungry," she said, "I'll set your food out on this little table."

"As a matter of fact, I'd rather leave, if it's all the same to you."

"You can leave whenever you like," she said.

"In that case, I'll leave now."

"Eat first," she said.

The boy had disappeared. She closed the door.

"I can see you're a bit worked up. Calm down. The food is lovely. The chef has prepared it just for you, your favourite meal."

"How does the chef know my favourite meal?" he said.

"You must have told us."

"I didn't."

"In any case, look. Steak and chips with fresh garden peas."

X looked at the plate. A sense of defeat came over him. He could eat and then insist she let him go. He was hungry. Perhaps it was sensible not to turn down a good meal. He needed energy after all. If he was going to use the knife to prise those screws out and climb across the roof, he required sustenance. He sat on the little stool before the table and tasted the steak. It was good quality and well-cooked and the chips, thick and browned were just as he liked them. It might have been his mother who had made the dinner. The first few mouthfuls stimulated his appetite. He wolfed the rest, as he did as a boy when he was called in from play and wanted to get out again quickly to join his pals. When he stood up and turned round , the young woman was naked on the bed.

"I'm just your type, aren't I?"

"What?"

"You like brunettes and brown eyes don't you?"

"Not particularly," he said, aware that his tone gave him away.

"That's why they sent me."

"Who?"

"I don't know. I do what I'm told."

"And you're told to do this?"

"Yes."

"That's no way to behave," he said, aware of his previous compliance.

"Why not?"

"You're supposed to do it because you want to, not because you're told to."

"I do want to."

"But you're obeying orders."

"I want to obey orders."

"You shouldn't."

"Why not?"

"You should think for yourself."

"I do. I think I should do what I'm ordered. Life is easier that way."

"Put your clothes on."

The young woman threw back her head and began to laugh in a raucous way which disturbed him. She was propped on her elbows, her legs swung open

"Oh," she said, looking at him, "that's the funniest thing I've ever heard," and she began to rub herself, groaning and arching. "Oh, come on, get inside me. I'm dying for it."

"I'm not in the mood," he said going over to the window to disguise his arousal.

"Do you want to do it this way?"

He resisted looking, but curiosity overcame him. She was on all fours, her rear high in the air, her face buried in a pillow. He was transfixed by the contours of her backside and her waist.

"I think you should come up my arse," she said, turning her face to him and then burying it once more.

When she had left, he took the knife from where he'd hidden it and went back to the window. It was growing dusk. The man was no longer pacing. A terrible sense of shame accompanied his diligent effort. Time and again the blade jumped from the slot, but he set it once again, pressed with all his might and tried to turn. By dint of hours of effort, he made the first screw shift a quarter turn. Delight surged through him. He was going to escape. It required only the will not to give up. Should he extract the first screw before starting on the second or might that make the fitting wobbly? It was more sensible to attack the second. If he could shift that one too, he was more or less sure of release. The second screw proved far more recalcitrant. Hours of effort didn't move it. His wrist was painful and he was thirsty. Should he ask for a beer or a coffee or tea? No, he would drink some water. Better not to bring anyone to the room, slight though the chance of them inspecting the window might be. He assumed there would be a glass or receptacle of some kind in the bathroom, but there was nothing. He ran the cold till it had lost all hint of warmth then put his mouth to the flow and sucked. The water was fresh and reviving. "That's better," he thought. "I can last for hours on water. Maybe a day or two. That should be enough." As he was leaving the bathroom, the phone buzzed.

"Yes?"

"Would you like something to drink?"

"No, thank you. I'm fine."

"Don't drink from the bathroom tap. We can provide sparkling water with ice and lemon."

"No, I'm quite all right, thank you."

Where was the camera? So, they'd seen him at the screws and done nothing. And they'd watched him with the young woman on the bed. Or was it only the bathroom which was surveyed? That wouldn't make sense. He scanned the corners, the window frame, the skirting boards, which he noticed were low and cheap looking. Probably they had some tiny device. He'd never find it. But if he worked in the dark? Surely they'd thought of that. Technology could do anything. Infra-red. Was that it? Why didn't she mention the window? Maybe in the corner he was out of range. Unlikely. Still, he wasn't going to give up. He returned to his work which brought him curious satisfaction. Yes, he would toil at this until he succeeded. What if the knife snapped? He'd order food. Strange they hadn't noticed the knife was missing. Or maybe they had. Were they playing a game? Would he open the window wide enough only to be apprehended? Was that a reason to give up? No, he had to try whatever he could. He laboured into the thick darkness, without any awareness of the time. When the second screw gave a fraction, he flopped onto the bed. Now it was merely a matter of going on. One screw at a time? No, simultaneously: a turn of one, then the other. That was the best solution. If he removed one the bracket might become unstable and prevent him loosening the other. He lay for what he thought was a few minutes. Getting up, he went to the bathroom and caught his dim reflection in the mirror. Who was he? He was himself and nothing to do with this place. He had a family. Or did he? He used to. And M, his girlfriend. Or was she? Was she wondering where he'd got to or was she already with someone else? No, it was true. He did have a life, he was simply set apart from it, for a while. Everything was done for him here. He was comfortable. He could have ordered food and drink, summoned a young woman. No doubt the gym was well-equipped. Maybe, once they were used to him, they'd let him stroll the grounds. That wouldn't be too bad. Perhaps he'd get to know people and the sense that it was all play-acting would disappear. A sudden surge in his chest made him hurry back to the screws. Though they had both turned they were stiff. His arm ached dreadfully. He tried his left hand, but it was too weak and awkward. He kept at the effort and the two screws lifted bit by bit until he was able to pull them out. Should he keep them? Why, when he was going to escape? But supposing he needed to retreat? It would be better to be able to replace them. He slipped them into his left-hand trouser pocket. The bracket no longer restricted the movement of the frame. He pushed it as wide as he could. Should he go headfirst? Yes, he would be able to reach the edge of the roof, grab it in both hands, drag himself onto it; but supposing his legs pulled him down. Would he be strong enough to hang on? No, feet first. On his front. He could hold onto the window frame while his legs found their way to the roof. There was a drainpipe. He could grab that. Or maybe to straddle the frame. Could he duck low enough, squeeze out, lean to the left, grab the edge of the roof? That seemed the best chance. He needed to think. He fell back on the bed, so comfortable he could have stripped off, climbed in and disappeared into sleep. In the morning, they would bring him a lovely breakfast. He could shower and shave. What then? The interview? Was it going to take place? If not, how would he spend the day. Perhaps they'd have something planned for him. Maybe another young woman. Suddenly aware of his tiredness, he sat up. He had done well. It was a matter now of not losing his nerve. Once on the roof it would be easy to orientate himself. Where was the front gate? He stood up and tried to create in his head a map of the way he'd got here. Surely the entrance was to his left?

Yes. Onto the roof, head left, as soon as he saw the fence and the gate, find a way down. That wouldn't be too difficult. Maybe there'd be a fire escape. There must be. It was the law. But did the law matter here? He recalled what the young woman had said.

It was thoroughly dark. He looked down. The sentry might have been there, still and silent. What did it matter? Once he was on the roof. Supposing he was armed. They wouldn't shoot him. Questions would be asked. The police would investigate. Unless they were powerless here. In any case, if they killed him, that was better than staying here. Was it, he reflected as he pushed his right leg through the opening, better to be dead than have a bed to sleep in, good food, comfort, women? He straddled the sill. The distance to the roof was too great. If he was to lean forward and pass his body through too, he might fall. Headlong. That would be death, but ignominious. No, to be shot was one thing, to fall out of incompetence quite another. If he could remove the window altogether, he could stand on the sill, reach for the drainpipe, get his hands on it and his feet against the wall, and from there it would be one step and a push to the roof.

He examined the hinges and levers with a heavy load on his stomach. With nothing but a knife? No. He would have to pass himself through the aperture feet first, stretch for the roof edge and push himself with enough force to avoid the chasm. How long would it take to hit the ground if he missed? Surely the force would kill him. Suppose not. Broken legs, a broken back and still conscious. Ach, was it worth it? For what? Freedom. Surely the risk of death was worth it. To live like this? He threw himself on the bed. If only one of the young women would appear and he could lose himself in sensual pleasure. Yet at the same time, he dreaded the prospect. Their coldness made him shiver. The outward act was satisfactory, in a way, but the inner experience was utterly lonely and bereft. He would rather do without, though he couldn't. The need arose and they exploited it. Was that true? How was it exploitation? They pampered him. Yes, but for their own ends. Which were what? He sat up. The window was wide. He needed only the courage to try.

He passed his feet through, his belly against the hard bar of the PVC frame, fishing for the roof, edging further a centimetre at a time till his right toe connected. Sliding himself rightwards, he waved his left leg till it hit the fascia. At once he was struck by how his physical strength failed to match his intention.; but if he pushed away hard, if he threw himself towards the asphalt. No. It wouldn't work, but could he drag himself back in? Yes, surely. Kick off with both feet. Yet he was so near. If he could grab the drainpipe. If it would hold. As if no longer in control, he pushed away and reached his right hand for the downspout. It was thicker than he'd imagined. His hand couldn't span it. Yet he gripped. Now the left. Yet if he let go of the frame would he fall? He needed to push away with just enough force to let him grab the downspout. Too much and his right hand might slip and his feet lose purchase. Once more, as if the decision had been made for him he pushed. His left hand grabbed. His feet were pulling towards him. He thrust against the downspout and threw his upper body rightwards landing with both hands on the asphalt roof his feet sliding to the edge. There was nothing to hold onto. He managed to dig his toes against the surface. His knees hit the same. He scrambled and was safe, two metres from the edge.

Standing, he could see the road, the tall lampposts casting white light, the cars passing at twenty second intervals. Freedom. He had liberated himself. It was simply a matter now of finding a way down and out. Was the guard down below? What if he was? If he came up he would fight him. He clenched his fists. Yes, he was young. He could dance. He could punch. He walked calmly to the far edge. There was no fire-escape. But there must be one. The authorities insisted. Yet did the authorities have sway here? He turned left and walked to the far corner. The air smelled good. That odour of evening he'd always loved. He paused to breathe deeply. Ah, the evening. The times he'd walked a girl home loving the scent of her and that of the coming night. There was a drain, a little, round grid towards which the roof sloped gently. He stopped, put his foot on it. Another step and he was able to look over. A fire escape. A metal affair, the steps heading one way then another, a platform between each section. So, they were answerable to the authorities. He could barely make out the ground in the dark, but it was easy to step over and take the first flight. He held the rail with his right hand and stepped steadily. No need to rush. Suppose one of the steps was loose. If he tripped. Take it easy. He was on the third flight when the guard appeared below, stopping at the base to light a cigarette. X crouched and nestled close to the wall. The guard took out his mobile. "How are you? All quiet. Usual patrol. Nothing ever happens. Meet me at the gate. Half an hour. I'll sneak you in. Come by the back road, stay close to the wall on the right, cameras aren't as good. Keep your head covered." So the gate would be open in half an hour. Could he slip through. If he might distract the guard while he was attending to his lover. He assumed that was who he'd spoken to. Perhaps they'd kiss. A few seconds of closed-eyes inattention. He was right above the guard watching him smoke. He could drop something on his head. The drain cover. He turned and stepped silently up the steps, bent his knees and tried to pull it loose. It was adhered. Why would they do that? What chance anyone would be on the roof and want to remove it? Yet here he was. If he slipped his fingers through the apertures maybe he would have the strength to pull it free. The four fingers of his right hand fit nicely and bending his thumb to grip he began to pull. There was a slight give. More force. If he pushed with his legs, the power of his thighs might make the difference. But his effort left the cover unmoved. Trying to pull his hand loose, he found his fingers stuck. They seemed to have swelled slightly. He moved left and right, forward and back but they were tight. If he stretched them and left them for a few minutes, perhaps they would shrink a little and pull free. Pulling must have warmed them. Letting them cool should be enough. But after five minutes there was still no movement. Lubricant. Up here? Was he going to have to call the guard? After all that effort? No. Long enough and his fingers would respond to the cold. It occurred to him his spittle might act as a minor lubricant. He gathered and spat, missed, tried again and by dint of a dozen aims managed to wet his fingers enough for a film to exist between his skin and the metal. By tiny degrees, he was able move his hand upwards, the middle joints jamming. If all he could do was tear his skin, he would have to. He yanked against the pain. Blood ran down the back of his hand. He flicked it, rooted for a tissue, dabbed with the scraps he found, lifted his fingers to his mouth, licked the blood and sucked at the raw articulations. Sidling without a noise to the edge he found the guard had disappeared. Now, what was the best? To find a way to the gate, conceal himself and hope for opportunity to escape unnoticed or to slip down the fire escape and search for a way over or under the fence? Perhaps the guard would let him go. Blackmail. "If you stop me, I'll report you." For what? He must be breaking some rule. Would there be a punishment? Logic dictated. Infraction of a rule must bring negative consequences or what is the rule for? Maybe he would lose his job? "Look, just let me out. I won't say anything. You've got what you want I've got what I want. "But if he was a jobsworth. After all, to work in such a place. All he would need to do was seize him and hand him over. Keep the woman hidden. Who would believe him?

How big was he? Maybe he could be overpowered. But there were two. Would the woman get involved? No. It would be better not to get caught up in a dispute or a fight. He must work with the dark. In silence. Unseen. Unheard. He could disappear. When they found he was gone, it would be too late. He would be back with his family. Why hadn't they come for him? They didn't know where he was. Had he told anyone? He couldn't recall.

At any moment the sentry might return, but the darkness was his friend. Once he was on the ground he could cleave close to wall, conceal himself in shadows. How high was the fence? He hadn't taken much notice. Why would you? Arriving for an interview you didn't want at a place you expected to leave in an hour or so. Still, it couldn't be too tall or he might have registered it. He was young. He could climb.

He took the steps one at a time, slowly, although he could easily have run down them in pairs. Why was he so afraid and cautious? Nothing terrible had happened to him. On the contrary, he'd been pampered. The only negative was his absence of choice. Who was to say if he pulled himself to his full height, showed he was capable and willing to stand up for himself, they wouldn't melt away. The guard was more interested in his woman, or what X assumed was his woman, than keeping the place secure. He was merely an employee. Why should he put his safety at risk? If X brandished his fists, the man might judge it politic to let him go. He could deny seeing him. The better outcome was to avoid all conflict. There was silence. He had space and time. He needed simply to keep his head.

He was on the penultimate section when he heard faint footsteps and panting. Pulling into the shadows, he stood erect and motionless as a young woman came into view from his right. He strained his eyes to make out her face but she didn't look like any of the women he'd met. If only it'd been the girl from the shower. He could have trotted down and spoken to her. They had been intimate, or at least experienced sexual contact. That would give him some rights. The idea struck him as odd. What rights? She wasn't his girlfriend. He had no essential contact with her, no emotional connection. Yet she had serviced him. The idea repulsed him. Yet the memory of the sensation pleased him. The young woman ran past the foot of the fire escape. Where could she be heading? Was she the guard's lover? He waited. Suppose just at the moment he put his feet on the ground the guard or she reappeared. He could climb back to the roof and wait. A few hours without activity should suggest safety. Was it cowardly? Was it cowardly to be cautious? Or was he rationalising his cowardice? No, a return to the roof simply meant he would have to come down the steps again. He had come this far by boldness. There was nothing to do but carry on. He listened. Neither footsteps nor panting. Perhaps she'd escaped. Like him, she might have been brought here on false pretences. Though that wasn't quite true. He came voluntarily. Though in response to an invitation he hadn't requested. Had she done the same? Perhaps she had scaled the fence and was on her way home. What was happening now in his home? His mother would be watching the television, perhaps wondering where he was. Maybe she had contacted his friends. His sister would have put her children to bed. Did they think he had gone to visit M? He hadn't told them he was no longer seeing her. His room would be empty, the little room at the back of the house overlooking the long garden. In a few hours he should be there. He continued his descent. At the base of the fire escape was a tarmac square. He stepped off it onto the grass and moved quickly left. The lights from the road risked illuminating him. As he moved, he scanned the fence which sat on a wall about a metre high. He could set his toes on the wall and pull himself up, fling one leg over the top of the fence, followed by the next. Why wait? There was perhaps too much light. He skipped across the grass, set his right foot on the edge of the wall, took hold of the metal spars of the fence and pulled himself up. A horizontal support ran close to the bottom. He was able to slip his toes between the uprights and secure a footing. The few extra inches made the next move easier. He withdrew his right foot, leant back to the full extent of his arms, flung his leg upwards and connecting with the upper strut, pulled with all his force. The tops of the spars were pointed which prevented him leaning over with his inert mass pressing down. By pushing hard with his right leg he was able to raise himself so he could bring his left foot up, balance it for a second on a spike, leap up and land with bent knees on the other side. The hard tarmac gave him a jolt. His joints hurt. He toppled to the right, saved himself on his right elbow and quickly got to his feet. His knees were painful but he judged it would soon fade. The shock of the pavement had run through his frame. He shook himself, brushed off his clothes and headed at a brisk pace for the main road.

There was no sign of the guard or the young woman. Why not run? He began at a trot, after fifty yards quickened and once he'd turned right towards the town, sprinted to feel his legs and lungs. The night was chilly and he regretted his coat, but he was away. It was two miles to the centre. He could catch a bus when he arrived at the roundabout where there was a pub and a few shops. He felt in his pocket for his card wallet. Nothing. He stopped. Had he taken it out? No. Maybe his mind was fooling him. Had he put it somewhere and forgotten. No. It had been removed. When? Money? None. He would have to walk. Still, two miles, he'd be there in twenty minutes. Beyond the industrial units a few sparse houses began to appear. There was a large, white, detached place, set back ten yards. The lights were on. He slowed. The urge to knock on the door was very strong. "Excuse me,

I wonder if you could help me. Could you possibly call someone for me? I've lost my phone and my wallet." To be invited. To sit on a sofa and be offered a drink. No. Press on. The houses became more numerous. A row of ex-council houses appeared, all with front gardens, each some distinctive feature. Who lived in them? People he would never know. He had an overwhelming desire to meet them. A man passed him, middle-aged, bald, short, in a hurry. "Evening," said X and the stranger returned the greeting. They could have gone to the pub together and engaged in conversation. At the roundabout, X experienced a relieving combination of excitement and belonging. He could have entered the *Green Man* if he'd had money. Or the little corner shop for a paper or a can of something. He stood looking at the bookmakers, still open and watched a couple leave the pub, cross the road and go in. He was now no more than a mile from the town. He could stroll it in fifteen minutes. A car, coming from the direction he'd just arrived, pulled up in front of him. For an instant he was puzzled, but bending to look at the driver, saw the young woman who had looked after him in the shower. The long, sleek white, electric car was obviously of the highest quality. Its comfort was appealing. The young woman looked at him as the window descended.

"Do you want a lift?"

"No, I like to walk."

"Are you hungry?"

He realised he was, though to that moment, he hadn't thought about it.

"No."

"You must be, you haven't eaten for five hours."

He thought of his last meal. Was it five hours ago? He couldn't have been accurate. What had he eaten?

"No, but I ate well."

"Hardly more than a snack. Get in, I know a nice place."

"No, thanks. I need the walk,"

He strode away. The car rolled along, smoothly beside him, the window down.

"What about a drink?"

"I'm fine."

The road descended steeply and rose again equally precipitously. He pushed hard as the car stayed by his side. The driver called something but he couldn't discern what. Down the hill, towards him, came a quartet of youths, dressed in black, their faces covered by balaclavas. As they neared, they bunched and one of them pulled a knife from under his hoodie. X saw the blade, longer than a good carving knife, and stopped. He could turn and run back up the incline he'd just come down, but they might catch him. Could he outrun four? They were ten years younger, though that didn't mean faster. He'd always been in the best five in his year at eight hundred metres, but if the lad with the knife was faster. Or he could fight. Against four? If he floored one. He'd never punched anyone, but he could swing.

"Get in!"

The car was stationary. The door opened. The youths surged forward. X ducked into the seat, the door closed automatically, the window rising at the same time. One of the lads leapt onto the bonnet. The driver gunned, he was thrown against the windscreen and rolled onto the road.

"Christ, he might bc dcad. Stop."

"We can't stop."

"You could be in real trouble."

"The police will be here in no time."

"How do they know?"

The car sped ahead well beyond the limit. As they turned the bend to the right in front of the grim old pub, now boarded up, where more youths were buzzing around the car park on electric bikes, a police van shot past them, its sirens wailing.

"How did they know?"

"Do you like Greek food?"

"I don't know?"

"You've never tried it?"

"I don't think so."

"Then we'll introduce you."

She pressed a key on the pad between the seats.

"Konstantinos, a table for two. We'll be there in five minutes."

Five minutes? Where was she taking him? A Greek restaurant five minutes away. He could think of nowhere in the direction she'd taken, away from the town, through the once notorious Honeysuckle Estate. There were no eateries there, except for a couple of fast-food places. The sleeping policemen slowed her. He wondered if he should take his chance and leap out, but it occurred to him he'd heard the click of the doors locking automatically. They passed the rows of social houses, all essentially alike. Improved by the council, they were decent little homes. There was nothing wrong with them from that point of view, he reflected, but they were looked down on by those in the more distinctive and expensive houses of the suburbs. Beyond the estate was

the road leading to the hills north of the town, territory he knew well from cycling the lanes at weekends. Yet in the dark, and given her speed and sudden changes of direction, he was quickly disorientated. He was sure they should soon pass the *Tray O' Cakes* café where he used to break his ride and read the paper, but it didn't appear.

All around was darkness, not even a light in a farmhouse. They went down a steep hill and over a narrow bridge with a river gurling beneath. That must surely be the Carwick, but he didn't recognise the bridge.

"Are we near the chair works?" he said.

"No."

They turned sharply to the left and there, a few yards from them, was a house, all lit up and inviting.

"I think I know that place," he said.

"Why should you?"

"I cycle here."

"Not here," she said.

"I think I do."

"You're confusing it with somewhere else."

The house was behind them and in front, the thick dark cut by the full beam.

"Where is this restaurant?"

"Way out in the wilds. Hardly anyone knows it."

"Is that good for business?"

"If you have a guaranteed clientele."

X began to wonder if he'd been wrong about the bridge and the house. Perhaps he'd never been here. The speed and the dark prevented him working out their route.

"Don't you use a satnav?"

"No need."

They were heading north, perhaps north-east. Trying to visualise the map, he judged they were among the hills and farms between his town and the next, smaller and ten miles distant, but there was nothing he recognised. The long climb up Sutton End for example, which had to be crossed to get anywhere. She'd said five minutes, but surely they'd been driving now for at least ten.

"We're going to be late," he said.

"Konstantinos will have the table ready."

At length, lights appeared. They turned into a wide gate and followed a long path, lit by little lamps at either side. What looked like a stately home came into view. They pulled up on the gravel. His door opened automatically as a man in a white shirt, black dickie bow and waistcoat greeted him.

"Your table is waiting, sir."

"Take him in," called the driver.

X was tempted to make a run, but to where? No doubt there would be security. Lights would scan the grounds. Maybe dogs were roaming.

"Where are we?"

"You're at the Greek restaurant, sir."

"Yes, but where is this. I thought I recognised where I was on the way."

"We don't advertise the location."

"No, but I'd just like to know."

"It's not for me to divulge, sir"

"Who is Konstantinos?" said X placing a hand on the man's arm.

"The proprietor."

X stopped and exerted a small, restraining pressure on his companion.

"I know. But who is he? And why is this place so secret?"

"I only work here, sir."

"Who comes here?"

"People like yourself."

"Always brought here?"

"I couldn't say."

"I was invited for an interview. I'd applied for no job. I've been detained against my will. Are you forced to be here?"

"I do my job, sir."

"Yes, but do you choose to?"

"It's a question I don't ask."

X looked over his shoulder.

"Where's she gone?"

"I've no idea. I'll take you to your table and she'll join you."

X pulled the employee to a halt.

"If you help me, I'll make it worth your while. When I go to the gents, order me a taxi. Give me your details and I'll transfer what you want into your bank."

"Taxis don't come here, sir."

The restaurant was bright and lively, almost all the tables occupied by well-dressed people having a good time. He'd expected the place to be small, quiet and depressed. So many people. Had they all arrived in the same way as him? As he was led to his table, people smiled or nodded, as if he was part of their society. He was placed in a corner from which he could survey the crowd. A waitress with long, beautifully brushed black hair came to his table, smiling\;

"Can I get you a drink while you wait, sir?"

"Yes. A beer."

"Draught or bottled?"

"Draught."

"We've got…"

"Any draught will do. What's your name?"

"Sorry, sir."

"I'd like to know your name."

"We don't get familiar with the clients, sir."

As she skipped to the bar, the woman who'd brought him crossed her, having changed her clothes into evening wear, her face made-up, her hair piled.

"Have you ordered a drink?"

"Beer."

"Good. Looked at the menu?"

She picked one from the pair propped between the condiments and handed it to him.

"We can stay the night here," she said.

"I'd rather go home."

"You'll be looked after well. I'll see to that."

She looked into his eyes and smiled, as if they were lovers. His response confused him. On the one hand he was repelled by the high-handed treatment, on the other, he noticed small but exciting attractions about her. Her lips, normally thin and pink, she'd painted red. Her ears, which he hadn't previously noticed, were small and close to her head. Her neck was very white and slender. Her dress revealed the top of her cleavage. He recalled how she'd offered herself in his room. The grossness of that was remote from the subtle effects of the moment.

"Shall we share a flatbread?"

"If you like."

"It's nice. With oregano. Ever had it?"

"No," he said.

"And some houmous. You've had that?"

"Of course."

"This isn't like the stuff you get in a tub from the supermarket."

"No?"

"Fresh and with a different consistency."

He nodded and looked from his menu to her eyes. She smiled, once again, as if they'd come here as a loving couple.

"Nice atmosphere, isn't it?"

"How did all these people get here?" he said.

"What do you mean?"

"Did they arrive like us?"

"They arrive anyway they like."

"I didn't."

"Isn't it a nice place?"

"Very."

"The food is lovely. And afterwards," she leaned across the table, raised her eyebrows.

X was stimulated but chilled. The thought of her offering herself to him naked, as previously, quickened his heart, but the mercenary nature of her offer, made him tense.

"Fancy the fried Kalamari?"

"I don't know."

"You haven't been very adventurous with food have you?"

"I'm not used to Greek."

"What about the pork skewer, that's quite predictable."

"Yes, I don't mind pork."

"Don't sound so enthusiastic," she said, looking at him sideways, "I hope you won't be so grudging later. Maybe the grilled octopus."

"The pork."

"It doesn't come with all eight legs," she said, laughing at her own witticism, placing her palm on her thorax, "it won't wrap them around you."

He surveyed the other customers who appeared happy and at ease. A woman of about thirty with black hair which she hooked over her ear each time it fell loose was talking animatedly to the three people at her table. She wore a red blouse, open at the neck. Her skin was dark. Perhaps she was Greek or Middle Eastern. Her teeth were very white and her conversation enhanced by her facial expressions and gestures. What she was talking about might be utterly trivial.

It was unlikely she was discussing interest rates or the future of NATO. Yet she was fascinating.

"What are you looking at?"

"Just the people."

The waitress brought the beer and his companion ordered a bottle of champagne.

"Do you like bubbly?"

"Not much, I prefer beer."

"I bet you've never had it."

"I may have. Once or twice."

"When?"

"At a wedding maybe."

"Whose?

"My sister's."

"Six years ago."

He looked up.

"How did you know?"

"Are her children doing well?"

"Fine. But how.."

"I'll order shall I? Leave it to me. A nice selection."

They were eating and drinking, X sipping his beer whose flavour he liked, and she emptying glasses of champagne remarkably speedily, when the pleasant atmosphere was disturbed. Two men in black evening dress, one tall and athletic, the other short, broad, bull-necked, moved in on a table, took the man and woman by the arms and lifted them from their seats. Both struggling, the woman was quickly overpowered by the taller, while the man forced his capturer backwards, the pair sprawling on the floor, the dinner guest kicking wildly as his oppressor held down his upper body. Oddly, from X's point of view, most of the diners continued eating, drinking and talking. The muscular intruder pinned his victim to the floor, his knee on the side of his head. Within thirty seconds, three more burly men had arrived, the prostrate diner was restrained, bundled away and it was as if there had been no disturbance.

"Poor bloke," said X, "and his wife. What was that for?"

"Oh, it's common for people who've had one too many to make a nuisance of themselves."

"But they weren't causing trouble."

"Of course they were, why would they be arrested else?"

"Arrested? Were those police officers?"

"Security."

"They have no power of arrest."

"The law is flexible."

"People enjoying a quiet meal can't be arrested and carted away like criminals."

"Unless they are criminals."

"What'll happen to them?"

"Don't worry. Here's our food."

The obliging waitress placed the dishes on the table. X noticed a mark on her wrist, as if she'd been gripped tightly. He was about to ask her about the disturbance when his companion said:

"Oh, thank you so much. That's lovely. Could I have another bottle of this?" And she held aloft the two thirds empty standard.

The unfamiliar food, X having restricted himself to the fast-food he'd grown used to in his youth, a few pizzas or, now and again, steak and chips, was welcome. He found it tasty and filling. The woman insisted on refills of his beer. The food and the alcohol, the warmth and the gentle atmosphere, in spite of the violent scene, relaxed him. He wanted to remain vigilant, almost on edge, but when the coffee arrived and he drank its delightful, slight bitterness through the chocolate-sprinkled froth, he felt himself ready to collapse in a an armchair or on a bed and, to wallow in the effects of his indulgence.

Wobbling on her high heels, having settled the bill, his companion led the way to the rear exit. They were immediately in a stairwell, cold and uninviting, concrete steps leading down to their left and up to their right. She took the ascending flight, pulling up her dress so her backside was revealed, the thin string disappearing. At the next turning, she stopped and leaned against the wall.

"We can do it here if you like."

"It's public."

"Who cares," she said.

"Aren't we going back to the car?"

"I'm ready for fucking not driving. Here, lick me."

She'd lifted her dress once more and tugged down her thong.

"Where are we going?"

"To bed, my sweet."

She laughed coldly and continued to climb. At the top of the next flight she pulled open a door which led onto a long corridor with doors regularly spaced on either side. The atmosphere was thoroughly changed. The air was warm, the walls were lined with embossed, expensive paper, the dark blue carpet was thick and accepting. A third of the way along she opened a door on the right and they entered a large bedroom at whose centre was a kingsize. Opposite were curtains the same colour as the landing carpet, down to the floor. The lighting was kindly. To the right was a wide dressing-table and a large mirror, immediately to the left a door which she opened and popping her head inside said:

"Bathroom. Very nice. For later."

In the little fridge concealed in the wardrobe she found gin and tonic.

"Don't you think you've had enough?"

"I've never had enough," she said in a flat, ugly tone. "Now, we need some music."

Slipping her dress to the floor but keeping on her shoes, she began to scan the channels as he stood by the bed wondering if he could escape. The door must be open. He could sprint the corridor, be down the stairs before she could come after him, but what then? Back through the restaurant? The heavies would get him. He'd be wrestled to the floor and dragged away.

She lighted on a channel playing raucous rock music.

"Oh, yes, that's the rhythm."

Glass in hand, she began to sway and gyrate, turned her back, bent double, rose, shook herself at him.

"Lie down, sweetie and take your clothes off."

"I need the bathroom."

"Don't be long. And no wanking."

He surveyed himself in the mirror. He was himself. Yet he was apart from himself. His features were as recognisable as usual. He was tall and fairly well-made. There was no reason he couldn't overpower her, gag her with tissues, tie her in sheets and make his exit. What was at the other end of the corridor? Maybe some simple way out, or if someone appeared from one of the other rooms, or if he knocked and explained:

"Excuse me, but I'm in danger."

The door opened.

"Finished?"

"Just a second."

"You've still got your clothes on."

"I'm just relieving myself."

"That's my job."

She went back to her dancing, leaving the door open.

To escape was hopeless while she was awake, or conscious. Surely if she drank enough she would pass out. He could then leave quietly, take his time. After all, he'd escaped from the other place. This couldn't be more difficult.

"Come on," she called.

He flushed.

To her request to get naked, he responded by taking off his jacket, tie and shoes and lying down, propped on a pillow.

"Refill," she said and went to the fridge.

She went on dancing, holding the glass, spilling little splashes.

"What do think of my thong?"

"Very nice."

"Shows off my charms."

"Yes."

"Disappears right up my arse."

"Yes."

"Take off your pants."

"You don't have to do this?"

"What?" she stopped.

"You don't have to do it."

"You don't like it?"

"I'm not saying that."

She began rocking her hips again.

"Don't you want me to suck your cock?"

"I'm saying you don't have to."

"I do."

"You should do what you want."

"I am."

"But not because you like me."

"How do you know?"

"It doesn't feel as if you do."

"How can you tell whether the woman sucking your cock likes you or not? Cock sucking is cock sucking."

"There's a difference."

"What?"

"I don't know. You can just tell."

"I do like you."

"You don't know me."

"What don't I know?"

"Virtually everything."

"Try me."

"What's my dad's name?"

"Malcolm."

"How do you know?"

"You're asking too many questions. Just get on with what's offered."

"Why am I being kept here?"

"You chose to come."

"I didn't."

"You responded to the invitation."

"Yes, for an interview."

"This is the interview."

"For what job?"

"That hasn't been decided."

"Why don't we talk?"

"I haven't absorbed all this booze to engage in chit-chat."

He found himself wondering why he was no longer seeing M. Sex with her was a calm beneath the excitement, but here he was starting to quiver.

"Any particular orifice?"

What had made him abruptly cut her off? It was some small comment she'd made, or the tone in which she'd made it; it had spooked him because it was redolent of an attitude he couldn't tolerate. It was a serious relationship. If they were going to spend a lifetime together, it would drive him mad. Why hadn't he discussed it? Did he feel he had no right to. She was what she was. He couldn't expect her to change.

"What's your name?" he said as his companion dropped her thong on the carpet.

"Mind you own business," she said, climbing on the bed and advancing on him on all fours.

An hour later she was unconscious beside him. To make sure she wouldn't rouse he talked into her ear, gave her a little poke on the shoulder. There was no doubt she was a beautiful young thing. Had her tenderness matched her beauty he might have felt warmly towards her. Now he could escape. There was no possibility of her coming round for hours. In any case, if she did, he would knock her cold. She'd still be drunk and a good upper cut would lay her flat.

He pulled on his clothes confidently and without excessive hurry. The door was locked. How had she done that? Or was it controlled from outside? She'd had a bag with her. A little, black thing on a thin strap. He searched for it, but it was nowhere obvious. At length he spotted a sliver of black beneath her pillow. Lifting its corner and sliding his hand beneath he felt its velvet on the tips of his fingers. Inside was a mobile phone and something which looked like a bank card. The mobile in his hand, he at once felt vulnerable. This would be tracked. Someone would know exactly where she was. Maybe they knew she was asleep and the phone in his hand. He went to the window. It was sealed. He could stamp on it. He went to the bathroom, filled the basin and immersed the device. Many were waterproof to a metre. Should he fill the bath? He took it from the water, dropped it into the toilet and flushed. It remained in the pit. He flushed again but this time plunged his hand into the water and shoved the phone as far as he could. When the sound of the cistern refilling stopped, there was no sign. What if she had used it to lock the door? Could he retrieve it?

At the door with the card in his hand, he slipped it into the slot and tried the handle. Some other way. He passed it back and forth. Nothing. After two minutes he stood tapping the card on the ends of his fingers, then idly tapped it three times above the lock, a green light flashed, he grabbed the handle and was in the corridor.

Which way? Back the restaurant, at least he knew where he was going. But the bouncers, or whatever they were. He looked in the opposite direction. The door at the end was surely a safety exit. There was no one and silence. He walked briskly and confidently, scanning for cameras. If they existed they were very discreet. A few meters from the end, a door on the left opened and a man stepped out, elderly but erect and dignified.

"Good evening," he said.

"Evening," said X.

"Are looking for your room?"

"No, I was on my way out."

"Oh, the exit's the other way. Through the restaurant."

"Yes, that's the way I came in, but I thought I'd try a different route."

"You can't get out this way."

"But there's a door."

"Never used. At least not by us."

"Who does use it?"

"I saw it open once."

"Well, I think I'll give it a try."

"It might set off an alarm."

"You think so?"

"I expect it would. Then they'd come running."

"Who?"

"Whoever's on duty."

"Have you been here long?" said X.

The man looked at him as if he'd asked something utterly mercenary.

"I've always been here."

"You were born here?"

"I don't know. What does it matter?"

"Wouldn't you like to leave?"

"Leave?"

"Yes, you could be free."

"I am free."

"So you could walk out if you want."

"No, they'd come after me."

"Then you aren't free."

"I am while I do what they say."

"Wouldn't you like to be free to disobey?"

"Then I would lose my privileges."

"But you'd gain your autonomy."

"What good would that be? They'd stop me."

X looked at the door. The old man had seen it open. It was in the nature of a door that it must open. What would be the use of a door which didn't? It wouldn't be a door. Perhaps it was masquerading as a door. On the other side there might be a sheer drop.

"If I can open this door will you come with me?"

"No, I'll have to report you."

"To whom?"

"Whoever's on duty."

"How would you find them?"

"I'd press the alarm."

"Which alarm?"

"Anyway, they're watching us. If you leave, they'll be after you. The dogs will be released."

Of course they were watching. Had they been doing so all along? Had they laughed as he struggled through the window? He scanned for cameras.

"They're hidden."

"Where?"

"They wouldn't be hidden if I knew."

"But you do know."

"Why should I?"

"You've been here so long. All your life. Let's go into your room."

"No, I want no trouble."

X placed his right hand on the man's shoulder and smiling and nodding as he squeezed hard whispered into his ear:

"I don't want to hurt you. Open the door. All I need is to see the inside of your room."

The old chap still had some strength, as if he might have spent a lifetime in physical work, but X was able to turn him to face his door and pulling him close to whisper:

"Open the door before I break your arm."

Inside, X let go and sat him on the bed.

"Are you okay?"

"I'm all right," said the old fellow rubbing his shoulder.

"Sorry. I didn't mean to do you any harm. There are no cameras in here are there."

"I don't know."

"Why would they spy on you? You spy on yourself. That's one of your privileges, isn't it?"

"I don't know. They don't explain."

"No, but I bet they've explained that. I'm sorry, but I'm going to have to take your card-key."

"Why?"

"Because it opens the door at the end of the corridor, doesn't it. Another privilege.

"You'll never get away. Why do you want to? Everything you need is here."

He offered the card.

"Thanks. Tell them I forced you."

X went swiftly from the room, waved the card over the handle, opened and stepped into a lift. Ground floor. Would they be there with dogs? The doors slid wide onto a foyer he didn't recognize. He took a pace forward, looked about him. The exit was to the right. He strode directly. A female voice behind him called:

"Can I help you, sir?"

He raised his right hand in a dismissive wave and was outside.

Total darkness ahead. Only the light from the doors behind him offered any illumination, but he couldn't stay where he was. For no reason, he ran to the right. He was on a hard surface. After a minute he veered to the left. It was surely sensible not to follow a straight line. At length his eyes adjusted. He could discern shapes. He collided with a bush and fell flat. Getting smartly to his feet he ventured into the shrubs. He could no longer run but had to feel his way. Thorns scratched his right hand. He felt the bark of a tree, tried to wrap his arms around it but unable to make his hands meet judged it must be tall and broad. There was comfort in being among the trees and plants which slowed him. He stood still for a short while, listening. Nothing. Weren't they coming after him? Perhaps they didn't need to. Was he was being surveyed even here, in the blackness and silence? Perhaps if he kept moving. He slipped his hand into his right trouser pocket and felt the key-card. Ah. He tossed it into the bushes and moved on quickly. An owl hooted. Something scurried in the undergrowth, but what was to fear? There were no fatal animals here. He had no idea where he was or which direction he was heading. He looked up but the trees and clouds obscured. Even if he could have seen the stars, he was unfamiliar with the constellations. He tripped over roots and collided with invisible branches. To press on slowly, carefully, never sure of what was coming next and with no certainty of where he would arrive was the only possibility.

His mobile was dead. He was without a means of measuring time. Maybe he'd walked for a few hours. Cold, hungry, tired, the desire to bed down was insistent, but he feared if he did the cold might strike through him, he might be incapable of going on once he woke. While he walked, he was producing heat. He was progressing. Or was he? To what? To where? It was blind progress which was maybe a road to catastrophe.

When the first light broke he was still in the woods. In a clearing a stag raised its antlers and stared at him. He stood still and the animal turned and trotted away. At least now he could identify the east and orientate himself. But which way did he need to go? South surely. Yet he'd been too disorientated on the way to the restaurant. He heard barking and turned in its direction, north-west. It was two hundred yards before he hit a path roughly made by walkers' boots. Something flashed by ahead of him. A cyclist. He hurried. There were long branches in his way and the grass was still tall. Here and there were patches of mud where animals had passed. Deer he assumed. He arrived at a tarmaced path, looked left and right. In both directions the surface swept away in a curve after twenty or thirty metres, to the right, leftwards, and the opposite way to the left. Which way? Another cyclist appeared, moving swiftly. He was dressed in cycling tights and a fluorescent top, his face covered by a warmer and his eyes protected by glasses beneath the peak of his aerodynamic helmet. X stepped forward and raised his right hand but the rider pulled clear and sped by. If two cyclists had come from that direction it suggested at least a village, or maybe no more than a house or two might not be too far away. He began to walk. His legs had stiffened. His calves felt tight. He needed food, a drink and a shower. As he neared the bend, a dog walker appeared. A woman about his own age in a long waterproof and brown boots, her Rhodesian ridgeback on an extending lead. When he was near enough for her to discern it, he smiled. She lowered her eyes. For a moment he thought he would walk by.

"Excuse me," he said.

She stopped and pulled the dog close. It barked and strained a little.

"Where do I get to," he said in as gentle a tone as he could, "if I go this way?"

"Mayflower Lane."

"Is there a village?"

"No."

"Is there a shop, or anything."

"No. There's a house. The old cottage by the stream."

"Ah. How far is the nearest village?"

"Well, if you go right at the gate, you'll come to Sandyforth."

"Is that far."

She looked in the direction.

"An hour by car, about."

"I see. Do you have a mobile phone?"

She stiffened and he saw a hint of outrage in her expression.

"No."

She yanked on the lead and paced away. He watched her go. The dog turned and barked as its lead was lengthened. He got out of the way.

He encountered no one else on his progress to the cottage. The stream ran behind it and was flowing fast and dark. He came down a steep slope, through the gate and the cottage was set back from the road by five metres, a low building, whitewashed but neglected. The gardens at the front and side were overgrown. There was a little, white wooden gate whose lower hinge was adrift. The lace curtains looked grey and tattered. Was this the only house? He looked around and could see nothing else. The path to the door had once been flagstones but was now broken pieces, uneven and unstable. Some attention had recently been paid to the door, a few dabs of white paint, probably primer and what appeared to be putty jammed untidily into straying joints. He knocked jauntily with his knuckles. A noise of shuffling but no one came. He knocked again. Silence. Should he call through the letter box? He turned his back on the door. Scanning the distance, he couldn't believe there was no other building. Surely a village of some kind, a little huddle of houses, maybe no more than three or four, must be nearby. He considered walking away, but this was a place where someone lived. There must be food, if nothing more than bread. A drink. A chair to sit in. Intending to knock once more, he faced the door. It was open and in the aperture was a tall man dressed in a suit and collar and tie. His clothes looked as if he'd slept in them for months. His collar was grubby. His face was clean-shaven but his sparse hair grew long over his ears. He stared down at X. His eyes were brown and hooded. His thin mouth was set. He held the edge of the door in his big right hand.

"Sorry to disturb you."

The man said nothing and remained still and impassive.

"I'm lost, you see. I..my car broke down and I walked. I had no idea where I was. I've walked all night. Through the woods and over the hills. I was wondering…"

The householder closed the door. X stood and looked at it for a few seconds, walked to the gate, returned and was about to knock when the man appeared round the corner of the house with a shotgun resting on his right forearm. He cocked his head, indicating X should go in the direction he'd just come from.

"It's okay. I'm not dangerous. I'll leave if you like. I was just hoping for something to eat and drink. And a mobile phone…"

The man thrust the barrel forward. X went in the direction indicated. At the side of the cottage was a dilapidated shed, the asphalt roofing felt hanging over the window and in front of its door, three big rats feeding from a full metal bowl. They showed no fear at his presence. At the rear was a narrow garden, sixty metres or more long, overgrown to inaccessibility. A few metres from the back door was a brick outhouse through whose open door of bare, warped planks X could see a toilet. He stopped, out of politeness. This wasn't his house. He shouldn't enter first. The man lifted the gun in a quick signal and he stepped into the kitchen. In the centre was a big farmhouse table with thick, turned legs on which a jumble of foodstuffs lay: bread, cheese, an open jar of jam, a litre plastic carton of milk, a box of cornflakes, a packet of peanuts whose contents had spilled, a plate of boiled ham, packets of *Oreo*, ginger nuts, custard creams, digestives, a chicken carcass stripped of half its meat, a plate of over-cooked sausages, cups, glasses containing various levels of unidentifiable liquids, a half empty bottle of whiskey. There were two, old straight-backed chairs, one at either end. An old-style, pale blue kitchenette, its drop-down open, stood in the far corner to the right. To the left was a gas cooker, piled with higgledy-piggledy pans. Beneath the window a sink jammed with crockery, cutlery and more pans. X stood still but the man nudged him with the butt and nodded in the direction of one of the chairs.

When X was seated, his host stood the shotgun by the side of the cooker, took matches from his pocket, lit the eye-level grill and taking two slices of white bread from the table, set them to toast. Meanwhile, he cleared some of the pans to expose a ring, filled an aluminium kettle and placed it on the burner. When the bread had browned he tossed it on the table, pushed the packet of butter towards X and handed him the open pot of jam.

"Thanks," but he was thinking of the animals feasting by the shed.

He spread the cold butter as best he could, but it clumped. The jam he applied thickly, and biting was delighted by its combination of sweet and tart, the blackcurrant tang inciting his hunger. The cook placed a plain black mug of tea and a packet of granulated white next to him. He picked up a dessert spoon from among the debris, wiped it on his sleeve. The occupant stood by the cooker, his hand on the gun. When X had finished the toast, he set two more slices under the grill.

"This is very good of you. I was very hungry. It's really great. Do you have a mobile?"

Slowly, moving to the table with deliberate steps, the man lifted the plate of sausages and set it in front of X who nodded and smiled. In spite of the outer blackness, X bit into the first as if it was perfectly prepared.

"Very good."

The provider watched him for a few seconds before setting the big bottle of tomato ketchup by his plate.

"Oh, yes. Good idea. Thanks."

He ate three, rubbed his belly.

"Pretty full."

The overseer picked up the gun and indicated the staircase, partly hidden by the kitchenette. X nodded.

"Okay. Do you live here alone? It's a nice place. I mean, a decent size and a lovely spot."

He mounted the bare, steep stairs which veered right and emerged onto a landing off which were five doors. The householder opened the one opposite, X entered, it closed and he heard a key turn in the lock. He knocked frantically.

"Sorry, but I need the toilet. Must have been the tea. Don't want to have to make a mess in your bedroom."

He heard the man's tread on the stairs. In the room was an unmade single bed, a dressing table whose mirror had fallen to the right and under the window three suitcases, side by side, their ends pushed against each other. Thinking at once that the building wasn't tall, he went to the window. Probably ten feet to the ground from the ledge. Hanging, he would need to drop only four feet. He could toss the bedclothes in a heap to break his fall. The old wooden windows were attached to the frames by angle iron. Once more he needed a screwdriver. He sat on the bed. What was in the suitcases? Old clothes? Maybe a woman's clothes. At the window were dirty lace curtains. The glass would be easy to break. What could he use? But by the time he'd removed all the shards, the man would be below with his gun. Yet he had only two barrels. Once they were done, he had to reload. That would give him time to leap or throw the bedding and leap. He was an old man. His sight might not be good. Maybe he suffered from macular degeneration and couldn't shoot straight. What could he use? The mirror was attached to the dressing table by butterfly nuts. He strained to remove the first. It wouldn't budge. A tool. Possibly in the suitcases. The first was held by thin, brown, leather straps. Its fasteners were stiff, but he manged to shove them aside and lift the lid on hundreds of black and white photographs. Taking a batch he sat on the bed. They were all of a young woman, very pretty, with dark hair and a very attractive figure. Her clothes identified the 1960s or 70s. She was in an armchair, beside a tree, on a bench, at a restaurant table, on a bed fully clothed, smoking, laughing, on a beach in a bikini which showed the extraordinary proportion of her figure, in a kitchen, among a group five girls of similar age, all with their arms around each other. Turning one of the pictures over, he found it marked "St Ives, 1970". He checked the rest and they were all registered in the same way. Beneath the piles of photos of her came images of children: babies, then toddlers, a girl and boy, she with dark hair in plaits, he a chubby, smiling boy, in one picture in a full football kit with a ball at his feet, his arms folded and a cheeky grin lighting his face. Then came pictures of them in school uniform, the girl as a brownie, the boy in a swimming costume on the side of a pool, a floating-ring round his waist. Teenagers, the girl in an evening gown, the boy astride a motorbike. The other two cases were filled with the same memorabilia. The final image was a gravestone whose inscription he couldn't read.

He lay on the bed. Why was the old bloke alone? Surely these were his children? The young woman must have been his wife. What a wonderfully beautiful young creature. He must have loved her passionately, at least if her character was half as charming. He forgot his need for a tool and drifted into imaginative speculation. When he roused, he regretted the wasted time. Going back to the dressing-table he took off his shoe and struck the butterfly nut with its heel. At length it budged. All four free, he lifted the mirror and carrying it by its two legs, launched it at the curtain and the glass. The lace billowed, the brittle glass split, and the mirror flew to the ground. He seized the pillow and began to use it to force out the shards. When the aperture was clear enough not to be fatal, he leaned out, expecting to see his host with the loaded gun at his shoulder. Nothing. Right leg first, he straddled the frame, hung on with his hands, pulled his left leg through and swung down. Pushing with his toes he let go, landed to his right, fell onto his arm and quickly got to his feet. Nothing broken or sprained. He headed for the gate but before he could reach it there came an explosion from inside. The door opened at his first push. The old man was on the floor, the gun beside him, his head a mass of blood. A fat, undaunted rat was chewing at his right hand.

X ran to the gate. How could he notify the authorities? If he waited, surely someone would come by. A car he could flag down. Yet there had been no sign of anyone. Suppose someone had heard the shot. But who? No, it was impossible. He needed to leave. No one could connect him. Except the woman. If she was questioned. She wouldn't recall much about him. They'd never track him. But it would be better if he could tell the police. His innocence would be easy to establish. No fingerprints or DNA on the gun.

Which way had the woman said the village was? Right. An hour by car. Thirty miles? He could walk at four an hour. Thirst. If he went back indoors and filled something with water. Suppose someone came. There was no one. He ventured back. Half a dozen rats were at the corpse. He emptied the milk carton in the sink, rinsed it and filled it with cold. Maybe some bread. He pushed four slices into his jacket pocket. That would keep him going. He'd be tired, but seven hours walking, a couple of pauses for rest, maybe a snooze. As he pulled the door closed, the car which had picked him up after his escape glided to a stop before the gate. His restaurant companion was at the wheel.

"Call the police," he shouted, running to her. "There's a bloke dead in there. Killed himself with a shotgun."

"Get in," she said coolly.

He sat in the passenger seat, half turned towards her.

"You have to inform the authorities."

"Best get you out of here."

"It was nothing to do with me."

"Who else was around?"

"Forensics will establish the facts in no time."

They were already speeding along the lane.

"What's that?" she said.

"Water."

"Thirsty?"

"Not yet."

"Let's go for a drink, eh?"

"There's a village. About an hour. But we'll be there in minutes at this pace. We can inform the authorities."

"That wouldn't look marvellous for you, would it? You turn up out of nowhere. You smash the old man's window. Next minute his head is blown off."

"That's circumstantial. The hard evidence will exonerate me."

"Who cares about hard evidence when a scapegoat is required?"

"That's not how the police operate."

"We'll keep the police out of it."

"But there's a man dead back there. The authorities have to know."

"By the time he's found, the rats will have stripped his bones."

They had turned off the A road and were following a narrow lane, centimetres at either side between the car and the hedges, yet her speed had barely decreased.

"Isn't this a bit reckless?"

"This lane is barely used."

"We only to need to meet one oncoming car."

"Don't worry. I'll keep you safe."

He tried to work out their direction, but the sky was too cloudy to be sure where the sun was. He was baffled that nothing seemed at all familiar. How far had they travelled to the restaurant? They took a steep hill downwards, crossed a shallow ford beside a stone house with a working water wheel where a child sat on the wall, kicking his heels against the granite.

"We should stop."

"They're simple people. They do no harm."

It occurred to him her speed might be to prevent him opening the door and throwing himself out, but when she had to brake for a hairpin and he pulled the latch, it was locked. No doubt they were heading back to the depot. Once again, he'd be in his room. She'd offer herself. The idea disgusted him. He'd be fed. There'd be all the entertainment he could crave. The thought diminished his spirits appallingly. Perhaps if he grabbed the wheel. Or seized her by the throat. A crash. He might be injured but perhaps he'd escape.

Hopelessness overcame him.

"We'll get you fed and watered, some new clothes, a shave and shower and a comfy bed."

The smile as she turned briefly to him might have been of genuine affection.

Back on an A road they quickly came to a busy junction. Within minutes they were on the outskirts of a town. He looked for a sign. Up ahead he could see one, too far to read, but before it came into focus, she took the brow of the road and turned right onto not much more than a track which dipped after a mile or so, took them through a tunnel and up into an underground car park.

"Home at last."

"Is this where I came for the interview?"

She laughed.

"Oh no, you've been accepted."

"But I was never interviewed."

"You've done nothing else."

She took his carton and bread which she handed to a man in uniform who arrived to assume the car keys. They went up in a lift to the fifth floor where they emerged into a huge space filled with people queuing for food and eating at tables.

"Is this a canteen?"

"You might call it that." I think you should eat first, though you look like a waif."

Hunger was less overwhelming than tiredness, but the offerings were highly tempting. He loaded his tray with soup, steak and chips, salad, sourdough bread, apple pie and yogurt, a coffee and sparkling water. They joined a table of six. He was seated next to a young woman who welcomed him with a charming smile. Nervous of his minder, he was reluctant to take her into his confidence, but when he was left unsupervised as she went to refill her tea, he set down his knife and fork.

"How did you come to be here?"

"Like everyone," she said.

"I was driven here."

  "Were you invited for an interview?"

"Yes, but not here."

  "No one comes here to be interviewed," she said. "We've all been accepted."

  "But I was never interviewed."

"We're interviewed all the time."

"What do you do here?"

"Enjoy ourselves."

"Don't you work?"

"What's the point of passing the interview and having to work?"

"I left an old man dead in a cottage. He shot himself. I wanted to tell the authorities."

"Did the rats eat him?"

"How did you know?"

"It always happens."

"Wouldn't you like to escape?"

"What for?"

"Well, to be free."

"Free of what?"

"Free to do what you choose."

She laughed.

"Who can do that? Anyway, tonight is the concert."

"What concert?"

He resumed eating as his companion returned. At length, the tables were removed, the false walls at each end withdrawn, tiered seating wheeled in. A stage rose up from the floor, busy people began to haul in equipment, scurry and organise.

"We need to get you spruced up."

He was taken up a narrow flight of stone stairs to a suite of rooms where he shaved and took a shower while the woman attended to her hair and make-up. On the double bed were laid out, underwear, a silk shirt striped in blue and grey, white trousers and a blue jacket.

"Oh, yes, you do look nice."

Being clean and dressed in the laundered clothes made him feel at ease, almost as if he belonged. A curious sense composed of defeat and acceptance began to gain him. He examined himself in the mirror. Some time ago, how long it would have been impossible to say, he'd accepted an invitation for an interview. Why, when he hadn't applied for a job? Perhaps he'd thought he was being "headhunted". But who could have known about him and what had he done that might be thought remarkable? Or had he thought it was a mistake he might as well make the best of? He had no recollection of his reasoning, or if in fact there'd been any. A letter arrived stipulating date time and venue. He turned up, since when he'd been serviced in the most attentive manner. What did he have to complain about?

"What is it we're going to hear?" he said.

"*All or Nothing.*"

"What's that?"

"You haven't heard of them?"

"No."

"They're the biggest sensation on the planet."

"So the public will be here?"

"Naturally."

"People will come and go as they wish?"

"Why shouldn't they?"

"Why can't I?"

"You've been chosen."

"By whom?"

"Those who make the decisions."

"Who are they?"

"What's the point of knowing?"

"It concerns me. I ought to know."

She laughed and came to straighten his jacket

"If we all knew about what concerns us the world would be in a fine mess."

"What's your name?"

"What would you like it to be?"

"I'd like it to be what it is."

"Well, choose. It's your freedom. I'll have whatever name appeals to you."

"What name did your parents give you?"

"My parents had no say in the matter."

"Why not?"

"Why should they?"

"Because they conceived you. They brought you up."

She turned back to her preparations and began brushing her hair.

"Don't be so sure."

"I have a sister."

"That's nice."

"Jean. I'll give you the same name."

"That's fine. Jean is a good name."

"What's my name?" he said.

"I don't want to know your name."

"I have a nickname."

"Really?"

"I've had it since I was a child."

"It's stuck."

"Saps."

"Saps?"

"Yes."

"How did you get that?"

"Because I was good at climbing for apples."

She laughed.

"Charming. Come on, we don't want to miss the opening."

She went before him and he noticed again how beautifully made she was, which stirred the old tenderness. He wondered if he should put his arm around her shoulder or tell her how lovely she looked. In the auditorium the seats were filling, mostly with young people. Some of the girls appeared no more than ten. There were t-shirts and hats marked *All or Nothing*. The audience was mostly female. Some of the boys seemed very young but more were thirteen or fourteen. The adults, apart from one or two, seemed to be accompanying. Yet he noticed one or two men, middle-aged or older, finding their way to their solitary seats.

Lasers, fireworks, raucous chords before the entrance of four girls he judged to be in their late teens. Each dressed differently, they all revealed large areas of flesh. At once the audience began to cheer, scream, gesticulate. Some held banners aloft, others waved posters they'd bought on the way in. The music began. Nothing but a regular, boring beat. The four began to sing and strut. They marched to one end of the stage, thrusting their hips, bending and shaking their breasts, marched to the other end doing the same. X was unable to discern the lyrics. They turned their backs , bent over, threw their microphones in the air. Four burly young men in tight white trousers and sleeveless vest appeared, The girls wrapped themselves around them. The men simulated sex. The song ended, the men walked off, their shoulders back and chests out. The audience responded wildly. Stewards held back girls who tried to storm the stage.

"What do you think?" X's companion asked.

"It's not to my taste."

"Why not?"

"Are they musicians or strippers?"

"They haven't taken off their clothes."

"No, but no one would be surprised if they did."

"What would be wrong with it?"

"Titillation."

"We all like to be titillated."

"We don't like to be manipulated."

"Everyone manipulates everyone to get what they want."

Her cynicism silenced him. He sat still watching the act. The second song had the same beat as the first. The melody was childish. It struck him there was a combination of childishness and depravity about the act. He looked around. Ten year-old girls were on their feet, cheering madly as the singers bent over showing their behinds to the spectators.

"I don't believe that."

"Just look," she said. "No one is forcing these people to be here. They're willingly manipulated. They identify with the band. It makes them feel good."

"Does it?"

"Of course."

"Why? Do they feel bad most of the time?."

"They want to belong."

"To what?"

"Anything."

After seven songs of the same variety came the interval.

"Shall we go?" she said.

"I thought you were enjoying it."

"It's not intended for me."

"But you like it."

"I like what it does."

"What does it do?"

"Keeps people quiet. Come on."

"Where are we going?"

"To have some fun of our own."

He was tempted to protest, to claim he wanted to see the rest of the show. A dread came over him at the thought of being alone with her, and in particular of sex. Above all, he must avoid that. She would come at him with her nakedness and availability, but he didn't know her. There was the base physical pleasure, of course, and he could feel himself rousing as the idea of it seeped in from a corner of his consciousness, but it was in the context of his confinement and being overwhelmed. Initiative was taken from him. No, at all costs that must be avoided.

She took him to a bar where the woman he'd sat next to at the meal was at a table with another woman and two men. He nodded and she responded.

"Maybe we can join them," he said, as his minder bought the drinks.

"I don't think so."

"I'd like to talk to her. She seems a nice woman."

She surveyed the table.

"Okay. We can talk to them for a few minutes."

They approached and the minder asked if they could squeeze in. X ensured he was next to the woman from the dinner. When the conversation gave him a chance, he said:

"I thought you were going to the concert."

"We'll watch the recording."

"I see. Is there any way," he whispered, "we could be alone."

She looked at him with slight alarm and amusement.

"To talk, I mean."

"We can talk now."

"Yes, but I want to know why I'm here."

"How will that help you?"

"I don't know, but it doesn't feel right, not knowing."

"Why should things feel right?"

He looked her in the eyes. She had a very kindly face, a barely perceptible smile.

"I don't like this nagging feeling."

"What feeling?"

"Not knowing, having things done for me, to me. I want to make my own choices."

"But they might be bad choices."

"I'd rather make my own bad choices than have my life ruled from the outside."

She laughed in a gentle, friendly manner.

"But that's not rational. If you made a bad choice which ruined your health. Think of it. Let those who know better make the decisions."

"Who are they?"

"We don't need to know."

"I do."

"It won't help you."

"Surely they can't be completely secret."

"Oh no," she laughed again, "they're remarkably open, except when it comes to what matters."

"What does matter?"

She leaned towards him.

"If you take my advice, you'll put self-preservation first. Comply and you'll be looked after. Don't ask questions."

"Doesn't it bother you?"

"What?"

"Having everything done to you."

"I've known nothing else."

"I have. Before I arrived for the interview I made my own decisions."

"About everything?"

"More or less."

"I can't imagine it."

A low thought ran through X's head.

"This woman, the one looking after me."

"Yes."

"She'll offer me sex."

"Yes."

"I don't like it."

"You don't like sex?"

"I don't like not being able to choose."

"Just enjoy it."

"But I don't, if you see what I mean. Beyond the basic friction." He paused. "Is that your partner?"

She shook her head.

"I'm with him for tonight. I've been with him before."

X fixed his look on her face which struck him as innocent and girlish.

"Do you love him?"

"If I'm told to."

"That's impossible."

"Is it?"

"Do you have sex with him?"

"If I'm required to."

"And is he required to say yes?"

"Yes. We do what we have to and they leave us alone."

"What if you don't?"

"It's impossible."

"What are you two whispering about?" said his minder.

"I was asking her about the concert."

"The speech is going to begin soon, then we'll fly out."

"Fly out?" said X.

"Yes."

"To where?"

"You'll see. Look, they're lowering the screen."

From the ceiling a huge screen was slowly descending, the lights were dimming, and the bar had ceased serving. The image of a young woman appeared, tall, wearing a tight dress which emphasised her hips and her breasts whose cleavage was visible. Her hair was perfectly coiffured, her face made up, her teeth gleamingly whitened. Everyone applauded. The young woman waited. When the noise had quelled she began:

I'm honoured to be with you tonight, to share with you my message of unity, prosperity and strength. (Applause). We are a great people and when we work together there is nothing we can't do. (Applause). The future is bright. We have great minds working for us. (Applause). We shall go from strength to strength. The genius of our people is all we need. (Applause). We have always been a people willing to make the effort. We have always overcome our problems. There are no problems we can't solve. (Applause). Nothing stands in the way of those who believe in themselves. We believe in ourselves. We always have. (Applause). There are splendid times ahead. We, your leaders are working for your well-being. From time to time, we have to deal with disrupters, but they will never disturb us. They have no power because the people are with us. The people have always been with us. The contentment doctrine has no real enemies. Our psychiatrists know how to handle those who are in the grip of delusions. We are the people of light. (Applause). You are wonderful people. I assure you we are with you. We know what you want and we will deliver it. Your dreams will be realised. Was it ever in doubt? We do not like doubters. Where there is doubt there is a challenge to the contentment doctrine which has brought so many advantages. So many happy people. You happy people. (Applause). Wherever we encounter doubt we will crush it. (Applause). Make no mistake we will hunt down the doubters and ensure they are dealt with. We have made great strides. We go forward. We always go forward. We have the technology. As for our foreign enemies, we will wipe them out. (Applause). We have the best weapons in the world. We have the best service people. They will destroy anyone who challenges us. People challenge us because they want what we've got. Jealousy is the motivation of our enemies. We will not allow them to succeed. They will be eliminated. (Applause). There are splendid times ahead. Nothing will stand in our way. We have a plan and we will implement it. Thank you for your efforts. You are great people. We are a great people. Nothing can prevent a great people from succeeding. You are happy people. Thank you. We will always support you. You are marvellous people. When we work together we are happy. We can be nothing but happy. We are moving upwards. Nothing else is possible. We will not have backsliders. We will deal with them. Be sure, we know how to deal with them. (Applause). We have experts. Great people. Brilliant people. The best in the world. Nothing can stop us. We go on and up. (Applause). The outsiders still threaten. (Booing). But we have secured our position. Soon we will take over. (Applause). We have billionaires on our side. Terrific people. We are ready to take over. We will take over. They say we can't, but we will. We are ready. Are you ready? (Cheers). The day is close now. We have worked for this. A long time. Now the time is come. We will take over…

X ceased to listen, instead looking around at the entranced faces, the nodding heads, the applause in unison.

"Good, isn't she?" said his minder.

"She hasn't said anything."

"That's her genius."

"It's some kind of madness."

"It's the coming reality."

"What's she talking about, taking over?"

"You'll be part of it."

"Of what?"

"The new regime."

"The contentment doctrine?"

"That's right. We've cultivated it, now it has to be unleashed."

"What's it supposed to be?"

"What you're experiencing."

"I'm not content."

"You will be. Come on."

"But she's still speaking."

"You don't want to listen. We're going."

She took him by the hand, got to her feet took her leave of the others and led him outside. Above them a helicopter was circling. She took a small torch from her bag and flashed a signal at which the aircraft banked, descended and landed on the roof opposite. They crossed a small courtyard, went through a side door and up seven flights. To reach the roof they had to climb a ladder and fit through a trapdoor. The downdraft almost knocked him over. Once aboard, he was told to fasten himself in and they lifted off powerfully into the night sky.

To ask where they were going seemed a betrayal of his anxiety. What was the point when he could do nothing about it? The destination was decided. The pilot didn't speak. His minder appeared sleepy. Never having been in a helicopter, he was exhilarated by the speed and the sensation of travelling through the darkness was thrilling. It occurred to him he knew nothing about navigation. No doubt it was all computerised: the pilot entered the end point and algorithms did the work. There was nothing to do but make the best of the journey, but he was slightly nauseous from the woman's speech, its highly unnerving vague promises and threats.

They flew into the dawn and landed in bright sunshine, swinging in from over a calm, pale blue sea whose small, gentle waves lapped onto white sand. Descending onto the tarmac, he began to sweat till his shirt was stuck to his torso. The light made him squint.

"Where are we?"

"By the sea," said his minder.

"Obviously, but where?"

"Does it matter?"

"I'm disorientated. I have no initiative, I'm flown out of my country by people I don't know. I need some reassurance."

She laughed.

"Come on, you'll have all you could desire."

For some time, he'd been aware of something close to panic . Now, absurdly, he was tempted to run away, or to begin fighting, to shout in protest, to try to attract the attention of anyone who might help him. Stilfing these impulses was extremely uncomfortable. His emotional state reminded him of his first day at primary school, or the times he was punished by his parents, particularly his father, who would deprive him of toys, send him to his room, deny him contact with his playmates. He had that curious sense he'd known on those occasion, of inner emptiness, as if his organs had desiccated. Into his mind came the image of himself arriving for the interview. Why had he been so relaxed? Why hadn't he recognised the oddity? Had he failed to turn up, he would be at home, he'd go to the pub to meet M and the old crowd. He'd listen to jazz and watch football. He'd visit his mother on Sunday. Or would he? Had it all changed? How did he know the world he'd left was still there? The woman had said in her oration that the "outsiders" were a threat. No doubt he was one of them. Everyone he knew was. These people hadn't taken over yet. He could still escape, get back to what he knew and warn everyone. But warn them of what? The "contentment doctrine". They'd think he was mad. Maybe he was. Perhaps his sanity had broken down and he was experiencing delusion. After all, hadn't there been a psychotic distant relative on his mother's side?

He was taken to a villa which overlooked the beach. The vast lounge was glass, floor to ceiling, on the beach side. The air conditioning brought relief from the gripping heat.

"I'll show you your room," she said.

She left him alone in more of an appartement than a room. Everything was of the highest standard, all perfectly clean and neat. The bathroom had a shower area where he cleaned himself under the gushing hot water. Maybe being fresh and clean-shaven would help him feel more normal. There was a dining area with a kitchen section. He examined the contents of the fridge, poured himself a glass of orange juice. In the wardrobe and the drawers were plentiful underwear, shirts, shorts, trousers, jackets, rainwear hats, shoes, sandals. Everything he tried was the right size. He chose long, white linen trousers because he thought they would protect his legs in undergrowth. He'd assumed they were on an island. He might have to swim for it. The idea made him collapse on the bed. How long had they been in the air? Hours. He was trapped. Unless he could find a boat. He had no seamanship skills, but he could try. Surely there would be an unattended boat somewhere. He could take himself off for a walk. Play calm and innocent. Yet hopelessness surged. He was lost. All he could do was comply.

As the thought hit him, there was a knock on the door and she entered.

"Oh, you do look handsome."

She sat beside him and ran her hand along his thigh, which made him tense and brought a sensation of distaste. Standing, she said:

"Do you want to see what I've got on under this?"

"I'd like to visit the island," he said, sitting up.

"Island?"

"I assumed it must be."

"No, we're on the edge of the continent. To the east there's three thousand kilometres to the border."

"Which continent?"

"It's immaterial. If we aren't getting into bed, let's go."

"Do you offer yourself to all men like this?"

"If I'm told to."

"By whom?"

"Those who give the orders."

"But, he said, taking her by the arm, "you can't live by orders."

She gently pulled her arm free.

"How else do we live?"

"We make our own choices."

"Or believe we do."

"If we believe we do, that's enough."

"Don't be silly," she said, as if talking to a child, "everything goes smoothly when we follow orders."

He followed her to the beach where people were lounging or playing games: volleyball, badminton, football, cricket. Dogs were chasing sticks and haring back to the owners. Children were running into the waves.

"There's the games room too," she said.

A large hall was full of people before screens or with headsets covering their eyes.

"Join in if you like."

He preferred to be outdoors. At least viewing the horizon gave him the idea of fleeing, but he felt she would leave him alone here. He might be able to talk to someone. If these people had arrived here in the same way as himself, they too might want to escape. He donned a headset and was at once transported. He was skiing impossibly fast down a precipitous slope among towering peaks. He flew over edges beneath which were great cavernous drops, but at every hazard, his skill was impeccable. After a short while, the scene switched: he was under water, diving to a huge wreck, swimming in and out of its creaking, rusting hulk. Sea creatures of all kinds swam by. Sharks surrounded him but he kicked away into safety. Corals of extraordinary vividness spread in abundance. When the scene changed once more, he was dancing salsa with a beautiful girl of eighteen or nineteen. How long he spent caught in these adventures he had no idea, but at length, his minder's hand rested on his right shoulder, she removed the headset and led him outside where a party was alive on the beach.

"Did you enjoy yourself."

"It was terrific," he said, and at once was aware that he'd let go of his unease.

He wanted to tell himself it hadn't been enjoyable, but in spite of all his previous anguish, it was true, he'd lost himself in the virtual expertise which flattered him and gave him agency and competence far beyond anything he'd known.

"Join in the party."

Mainly young people, many wearing the minimum for decency, were dancing, chatting, lying on the sand, drinking, smoking spliffs. Here was an opportunity to mingle, to maybe find a fellow spirit which might be the prelude to escape. Yet part of him was growing weary of the effort. Why not fall in and enjoy the event. A few drinks, a chat to a welcoming girl, or striking up a friendship with a congenial bloke, that at least would be a relief from the tension. He couldn't kill off altogether his desire to be away, but it had grown distant and a will to self-abandonment was creeping. After all, it was one night. Tomorrow he would be icy sober and could rediscover his determination.

He asked the young lad behind the makeshift bar for a beer which was handed to him in a tall, slender glass. The cooled, autumnal-hued drink went down easily and the taste reminded him of *The Joiner's Arms* and his friends; those Friday and Saturday nights when they were packed shoulder to shoulder. He could enjoy himself here in the same way. Everyone was in a sweet mood. He wandered through the crowd. Girls in skimpy bikinis were at every turn and the loveliness of their youth, nature's temptation, the extraordinary gift which trumps all others, stimulated his impulse to relax. His glass quickly empty he returned to the bar. The cornucopia was seductive. He could drink as much as he liked. As he turned away, a girl offered him a tray full of tit-bits: little squares of salmon and cream cheese like the ones his mother sometimes served; blinis with caviar; miniature samosas; olives; humous, tzatziki; tomato slices with feta. She was ten centimetres smaller, dark with glistening brown eyes and a guileless smile. Her skin was tanned and she wore a white bikini.

"Oh, lovely," he said.

"I haven't seen you before."

"No, I've just arrived."

"Great. In time for the party."

"Yes. Have you been here long?"

"At the party?"

"No, in this place."

"I was born here."

"I see. Your parents too?"

"Maybe."

"What's your name?"

"What do you want it to be?"

He was stunned for a moment and knew it must have been apparent.

"You must have a name."

"Yes. But I change it to suit the people I meet.."

"What do your parents call you?"

"I don't see my parents."

"Do you have sisters or brothers."

"I may have. I don't know. Anyway, I don't see them."

"What do your friends call you?"

"Whatever they like. Have some more to eat."

He was glad of the food which was well-prepared and tasty. The young girl was smiling at him obligingly. He couldn't but notice her attractiveness, especially as she was almost naked. The disturbance the matter of her name caused him fought with his pleasure. What did it matter? If that was the norm among these people, why shouldn't he give her any name he fancied? The idea was absurd, but perhaps only because he wasn't accustomed to it. All the same, a name was a simple device: how could people be identified if their names were changing from day to day, hour to hour, minute to minute? Did he identify himself by his name? In a way, he did, because his identity lay with other people. Without other people he would go mad. All the people who knew him had their particular view and all those combined, together with his conception of himself, constituted his identity.

"These are very nice," he said.

"I know. Moreish. Come on, let's dance."

He finished his drink and went with her into the crowd. They were pushed together. He put his hands on her waist whose curve aroused him. Before long, they were kissing and her warm soft mouth felt like belonging. She led him away to a quiet cove where, in the dark, they were undisturbed. He sat with his back against the cliff face looking out at the dark ocean, whichever one it was.

"Have you ever tried to escape?" he said.

"Escape what?"

"This."

"What's wrong with this?"

"What do you do?"

"What do you mean?"

"Do you work?"

"If I'm told to."

"At what?"

"Whatever I'm told to."

"At the moment."

"I programme."

"What kind of programmes?"

"Weapons."

"To be used against whom?"

"I don't know. Maybe the outsiders."

"Who are the outsiders?"

"Anyone who doesn't agree."

"Are you happy doing that?"

"I have a good time."

"Yes, but are you happy."

"I don't know. I have a good time. I live well. I don't ask myself any questions."

"I was brought here," he said, moving towards her. "I was called for an interview and since then everything that has happened to me has been against my will."

"Including what we just did?"

"No, not that. But being at the party. Everything."

"You liked the food and the drink, and me."

"Yes, of course I like you."

"Well, enjoy yourself. You're being given the chance."

"I'm not enjoying myself. Or at least, only in an odd way. I need to choose."

"Choose what?"

"Everything."

"That's silly. You have to go along with things. If everyone chose everything, there'd be chaos."

Would there? He couldn't see, one way or another. Most people would choose according to their natures and most natures are similar. What do the differences matter? I choose coffee you choose tea. That's not chaos. Maybe she was right and there was something he couldn't see.

"What is it you go along with?"

"Whatever I'm told to do."

"Who tells you?"

"Whoever. I get messages."

"You must know who from."

"The machine decides."

"What machine?"

"I don't know. Nobody does. The machine. That's all we know."

"How do you know the machine decides?"

"The machine tells us."

"But somebody must be running the machine."

"Of course."

"What gives them the right."

"The right? They just do. They look after us."

"Even if you disagree"

"Who would disagree with a nice life?"

"How can it be nice if you're controlled?"

"If we weren't, who knows what would happen?"

"At least you'd be free."

"To do what?"

"What you know to be right."

"The machine knows better than we do."

"Suppose you could break free. No longer rely on the machine. You might find it liberating."

"I might get caught."

"Then what?"

"No one escapes. The machine knows everything."

"I escaped."

"Why are you here then?"

"She picked me up. But I got away. I was in a room, in a building, back in F, where I come from. I got out of a window and across countryside. I did it once. We could do it."

"I don't want to."

"Do you like your life?"

"It's the only one I know."

He had known two and this was the lesser.

"Who are the outsiders?"

"People who want to destroy us."

"Have you met them?"

"No one has."

"How do you know they want to destroy you?"

"That's what we're told?"

"But who are they, exactly?"

"Anyone other than us."

"That includes me."

"It did till you arrived amongst us."

"I didn't arrive I was summoned."

"That's a good sign. They wanted you. The machine has picked you out."

"It's made a bad choice."

She laughed.

"It never does."

"If there's choice, there can always be a bad one. If the machine can't make a bad choice, it can't choose, which means it can't have chosen me."

"Well, it has. Let's go back to the party."

What had been irresistible a little while earlier now repulsed him. She was the same slim, pretty girl, her eyes were as bright, her hands as elegant, her smile as charming, but he could no longer see her as a person. She was the embodiment of whatever had taken him from his former, pleasant life. Yet was it pleasant? Wasn't it full of irritation? Hadn't he lost his job stupidly? Hadn't work been a nuisance he would have liked to escape? Wasn't there trouble in his relationship with M? Did she drive him mad being keen one day and beyond reach the next? Wasn't his dad becoming more and more difficult and distant? All this and more was true, but it was a real life, while this was a dumb show.

He regretted talking frankly to the girl. Perhaps she would betray him, and if it were true the machine knew everything, presumably he was now a marked man.

"I'll get myself another beer. Do you want anything?"

"A large white wine, please."

He left her dancing with a group of girls who seemed to be having a wonderful time, but to him they seemed like puppets. His minder joined him at the bar.

"What have you been up to?" she said.

"Don't you know?"

"As a matter of fact, we do."

"We?"

"She's very pretty, isn't she?"

"Very."

"You enjoyed her."

"These things happen," he said, his mind split between shame and dignity.

"That's just as it should be."

"What is?"

"That you enjoy yourself."

He thought he had but now he found he hadn't. Of course, the act itself had been pleasurable, but at an animal level. Now he could view it more or less objectively, it was objectionable. She hadn't forced him, or even cajoled him too wantonly. He'd attributed to the liaison the same value he applied to his sexual relations with M: tender feeling, privacy, intimacy. Now it seemed, his private acts were the business of those in control. How foolish to think the girl might have agreed to escape. Would anyone? Presumably there were others who had got here in the same way he had. Maybe they'd been here so long they'd forgotten.

"I'd enjoy some time to myself," he said.

"By all means."

"I'm ready to sleep."

"Come on, I'll take you to your room."

"It's fine. I'll go alone."

"You know the way."

"Yes."

"You have the key?"

He looked at her questioningly. She took the card-key from her bag.

"I'll join you in an hour."

"No, I'm tired. I'll finish my beer and go to bed."

"As you wish."

In his apartment he switched on the tv and tried to find a news channel, but there was nothing but films, sport, game shows, documentaries. He found one about history. Perhaps he could discover something about where he was and how it came into being, but it was the history of his normality, the stuff he might have learned in school, accompanied by a derogatory commentary. This was the "before time", yet before what wasn't specified. One section dealt with London in the 1980s, when he'd spent time there because he had friends who were students at LSE, University College and Goldsmiths. He paused the film, rewound, watched the same few minutes over and over. Yes, that was Ladbroke Grove where P had a flat. He'd stayed there many times. The commentary disdained the period as one of chaos. Images of anti-poll-tax demonstrators were accompanied by derisory references to ignorance, unruliness, lack of control. He'd never been on a demonstration. His interest in politics was peripheral, his abiding feeling was of being misled and manipulated; but now he wished he'd been more engaged. What had he felt about the Poll Tax for example? Not enough anger to join a protest. Now, if he could protest against the machine, he'd lead the march.

The tv off, in bed, his anxiety was his minder would come and find him. No doubt she would be able to open the door. Supposing she got into bed. If he rejected her out of hand, what might she do? Perhaps he should play along. By feigning compliance maybe he could find out more and work out how to defeat the machine. Yet the idea was absurd. He was alone. He lay awake a long time, his heart racing. The next he knew, his minder was beside the bed with a tray of breakfast, dressed in an unbelted blue silk dressing gown .

"Sleep well?"

"Yes."

"Good. Today is the tennis tournament."

"Oh?"

"We've got prime tickets. Everyone will be there. You'll be amongst the elite."

As he ate, relishing the well-prepared and presented food, especially the toast which was grilled lightly and covered with a thin film of butter just as he liked, she took off her gown and slipped in beside him. He ate slowly, wondering how he could extricate himself. Her presence was burdensome, her nakedness a threat. Was she going to insist on sex? It was outrageous and bizarre. Why did women here behave in this way? He sliced into the eggs benedict. The smoked salmon was delicate and the bacon unsalted, to his taste. How did they know? The idea almost put him off the food.

When he'd finished and set the little, white, China coffee cup down on its saucer, she rolled towards him.

"Put the tray on the floor. We haven't got long."

"I need the bathroom."

"Don't take too long."

"Why do you want to have sex with me?"

"Who says I want to?"

"Why would you, otherwise?"

"I do what I'm told."

"You're told to have sex?"

"What I'm told is not for you to know."

"Why not, if it concerns me?"

"If everyone told others what they've been told to do, there would be chaos."

"People here seem to have a great fear of chaos."

"Life is easier if people do what they're told."

"But who tells them?"

"You know."

"Do I?"

"The girl told you last night."

"The machine?"

"That's right."

"Where is the machine?"

She laughed and folded back the sheet so her breasts were on show. Beautiful and appealing, he was almost seduced, but the dragging weight of her intrusiveness and the madness of her obeying an external command, subdued tender feeling.

"Everywhere."

"There must be some central location or set of locations."

"Oh, no. They've overcome those problems."

"How do you get your instructions?"

"We don't. We do what we feel like doing."

"But you said the machine gives you orders."

"That's the beauty. We experience ourselves as choosing but we are merely obeying."

"How do you know?"

"Some of us have to be trained in the ways of the machine, in case things go wrong. But they never do, except in small ways. Be quick."

He went into the bathroom, locked the door and immediately looked for a way of escape. There was no window, but as soon as the door was locked a fan began to whirr. He climbed onto the side of the bath to take a look. The outer grill was far too small to hide an aperture wide enough to climb through. Maybe with time and a tool he could scrape out an access, but for the moment he was trapped. Perhaps the simplest was to get into bed and have done. The idea repelled him. He began to feel bad about having enjoyed the breakfast. It had been prepared for him. It had been ideal and he had fallen for it. They knew his tastes. They had responded to them minutely and he had complied. By eating the food he'd put himself in their power. Perhaps he could resist arousal, but he knew that was hopeless. She would employ whatever means she needed. He could feign illness, stick his fingers down his throat. He shaved, showered and dried himself. Appearing with the towel round his waist he said:

"I'm not having sex."

"Aren't you?"

"No."

She peeled the covers off her and opened her legs.

"Don't be a spoil sport."

"It disgusts me."

"No, it doesn't."

She crawled quickly across the bed, pulled away his towel and began to kiss him, holding him tightly by the waist. He pulled away.

"That doesn't look like disgust."

"Let's get dressed."

She sat on the edge of the bed, leaning back.

"We know what it is. Women don't behave like this. Of course not ,where you've come from, but this is different. My job is to please you, and we know you're resisting because it feels odd. It won't as time moves on. And there's no point in thinking you might make your escape by the bathroom. Even if you did get out of here, we'd pick you up in minutes. Get dressed. I'll be back in a jiffy."

She slipped on the gown and was gone.

He was taken to a huge arena. Long queues waited at the entrances but he was spirited past the security and into a high box overlooking a pristine court.

"See the woman in the blue dress, just there to your left?"

"Yes."

"She's our greatest film actor. And next to her is the head of internal security."

He estimated there were two thousand or so seats around this one court.

"How many courts are there?" he said.

"About thirty. Only a dozen like this. The rest are peripheral."

Maybe there were fifty thousand in the complex. Surely, in spite of all their surveillance, it would be possible to lose himself here, and if he could sneak out...He wondered if at that moment she knew what he was thinking. If so, maybe she needed to be near to pick up his thoughts. He toyed with leaving his seat before the match started but judged it would be better to go between games. If he could change places with someone in the crowd. Maybe he could overpower some bloke, put on his clothes, walk away with his cards and documents. Yes, they might have access to his mind, they might be able to track him everywhere and know what he was thinking, but he could make it a little harder for them.

The match was between two of the highest ranking male players and the crowd partisan. There was great cheering and whooping as points were won. He waited till the seventh game because he recalled from having played himself the talk of "the vital seventh".

"Be back in a sec."

"Where are you going?"

"To the gents."

"Bring me back a wine, will you."

"Sure."

Once down the stairs and into the area between the courts, he was in the middle of a milling, good-natured crowd. They were dressed for the pounding sun and to impress. He wandered into a pavilion where people were queuing for food and drink. Perhaps if he went to the peripheral courts he would find some out of the way exit, but as he left the pavilion and turned right where the sign indicated courts 15 to 20, he passed the main entrance. Security men were checking the bags of the few people arriving. The lane next to them was open. No security people were in evidence. His desire was to bolt for it, to pelt as fast as his legs would carry him away from the venue, but he sauntered with his hands in his pockets, the sun hat his minder had given him over his eyes.

"Excuse me, sir."

"Yes."

"Can I see your pass?"

"I'm leaving."

"I know, but I need to see your pass."

"Why, I'm leaving?"

"I appreciate that, sir, but it's security you see."

"Well, I've left my pass with the person I arrived with. I could go and get it, but I don't want to disturb people."

"No, I understand, but I can't let anyone leave without seeing their pass. That's the rule, sir."

"Okay. Fine. I'll be back in a minute."

He took the path to the outer courts. Behind the high hedge which set the boundary, were splendid houses and at their upper windows, people enjoying the spectacle for free. Of course, the inner courts where the elite players performed where hidden. The crowd thinned. Mostly, the courts were being used for practice. On one, there was a little crowd of principally young fans. A dark-haired, big-hitting player seemed to have their attention. X paused to watch. After a few minutes, the player approached the youngsters at the fence, batted a few balls over to them and signed what they passed over. Walking on, X noticed some of the knocking-up players had discarded track suit bottoms, hoodies, baseball, caps towels and racquets at the entrances. How hard might it be to sneak something away and disguise himself? He wandered a narrow path between courts twelve and thirteen, turned the corner to approach the door. A security guard appeared.

"Can I help you, sir?" she said.

"I was trying to get a better view."

"You can watch from the side or the other end. This section is reserved for players and their teams."

"My apologies. Nice work for you, getting to see the players close up."

"I don't mind it."

"No, I wouldn't either."

"Have you got tickets for the elite courts?"

He sensed an opportunity.

"Yes. As a matter of fact, we're in one of the best boxes. What's her name, it's slipped my mind, you know the film star with long dark hair, Spanish-looking.."

"Oh, the one who was in *The Machine Decides*?"

"Yes, that's her, she's sitting close to us. Various celebrities and high-ranking folk."

"That's nice."

"Is that your office, then?" he said indicating the green shed she'd emerged from.

"I wouldn't call it an office. I can sit down and there's a kettle and a microwave."

"Luxury. Would it be cheeky of me to ask for a brew?"

"Can't I'm afraid. Staff only. Sorry, but you'll have to move along."

"Of course. Sorry to have troubled you."

"No, that's fine."

He made his way back and she retreated to her hut. He wondered if he'd been too polite and easily deterred. From his experience so far, he might have been able to inveigle himself into her confidence. After all, surely the girl at the party hadn't been told to be intimate. Or had she?

He passed a couple of players on their way back from practice. It would be easy, with a bit of gear to pass himself off as a competitor, then there would surely be no restriction on leaving. Perhaps the most remote courts would be best and maybe there he'd find some obscure exit. At the extreme edge of the complex was a pair of courts, one occupied the other free. Two girls aged about nineteen were whacking balls back and forth. There appeared to be no coaches present. He slipped the bar, pushed open the door and nipped onto the spare court. When a stray ball came his way, he ran to it and threw it to the girl to his right.

"Thanks."

"That's okay. I'm an experienced ball-boy."

They didn't object as he gathered the balls and tossed them. If they are leaving the complex, he reasoned, I could tag along. Presumably they won't object. After half an hour of chasing and throwing, he saw someone at the far corner waving. His minder. He waved in return, hoping she might leave him, but she came to the netting and called to him:

"Come on. The top seed is about to play."

 He would have liked to have left the court, given her a punch and made a run for it, but no doubt a posse of security people would have been on him in seconds.

"Enjoying yourself?" she said.

"Yes."

"Lovely girls, aren't they?"

"I was paying attention to their ground shots."

She laughed.

"Oh, come on. Those little skirts and their young thighs. You fancied your chances."

"I suppose it all depends, he said, "on what they've been told to do."

"They've been told to please the masses. A little leeway is allowed."

Reseated, they watched the top seed, a superbly athletic man of twenty-five or so play extraordinary shots, scurry with stunning speed and break his opponents serve in the third game.

"Marvellous, isn't he?"

"Amazing. Has he been ordered to do it?"

"He was sensational by the time he was four. He wouldn't have chosen anything else."

"But could he?"

He turned to look at her and she met his eyes.

"It's a question with no meaning. His inclinations and what is required tallied perfectly."

"Do yours?"

"We aren't all so lucky, but we adjust."

"What happens if you don't, or can't."

"That never happens."

The top seed triumphed in three. She took him to a exclusive pavilion where champagne was unlimited and long tables covered in pristine, blue cloths were spread with a gorgeous selection of food. After the first few glasses, a desire to get drunk came over him. It seemed somewhat reckless, given his lack of agency: why make himself even less in control? But in choosing to drink himself into a stupor he was at least taking some control, and as the sense of self-abandonment increased, he became less anxious and intent. The last thing he recalled was falling off a bar stool, spilling his drink and lying on the carpet laughing. He woke in a huge bed in a room he didn't recognise. His head was pounding and his mouth dry. On the bedside table were pain killers and a litre of sparkling water. He filled a glass, downed it, filled another, took two tablets and put himself under the shower.

His clothes were in a crumple by the bed. In the wardrobe were new trousers, shirts, shorts. In the drawers, underwear, knitwear. He tried on a few items. Perfect fit. He brushed his hair standing in front of the long, wardrobe mirror. There was a knock and a young woman entered with food.

"Morning, sir."

"Hello."

He inspected the breakfast: exactly what he had eaten last time.

"Did you make this?" he asked.

"No, I just deliver."

"Who's the chef?"

"I don't know their names."

"Fancy a cup of coffee?" he said, pouring.

"I'm not allowed."

"Who's going to stop you?"

"No one, but I'm not allowed."

"That doesn't make sense. If no one will stop you, you're allowed to do whatever you choose."

"Yes, but I can't choose to drink coffee with you."

"Why not?"

"Because it's not allowed."

"Well, let's change the rules."

"That's impossible."

"No. Some rules can't be changed. We're all going to die, that's a biological rule, but that you can't drink coffee with me is a rule someone has imposed, so we can change it. In fact, I change it here and now."

He poured, added milk and held out the cup.

"Sugar?"

"I can't."

"You can, honestly you can. Just take the cup from me."

"Sorry," she said, turned on her heels and left.

His momentary instinct was to fling the cup at the wall, but that would have been mere impotent petulance. It wouldn't assist his effort to escape. He was alone in this new place. The sensible course was to look for something they'd neglected. The windows were sealed., the air conditioning perfect. No doubt controlled by the machine. He assumed he was in a hotel. Maybe it was worth prowling the corridors. Yet he was sure he was being watched and listened to. There was no need for the minder to be with him every minute. What had become of his mobile? Had he lost it, left it behind or had it been taken? Why would they do that? It would help them keep an eye on him. Their surveillance made escape almost impossible. Why did he think almost? There must be a failure somewhere. In any case, if he gave in, he would cease to be himself. Somehow, he would be programmed. If the only way to avoid being controlled was to be destroyed, that would have to be.

He opened the door and was surprised to find a landing. He took a few steps forward and paused. Clearly this was a house. There were four or five bedrooms. He tried all the doors. The rooms were like the one he'd woken in, all with large, private bathrooms. None showed signs of occupancy. The stairs doubled back and led to an enormous lounge one wall of which was sliding glass doors overlooking a garden which extended beyond his view. A garden ? There ought to be some weak point: a gap in a hedge, a broken fence panel, something to climb on inadvertently left out. The doors were locked. Surely the key would be somewhere. He searched the kitchen drawers and cupboards. There was a study or office with a handsome desk and bookcase with a couple of hundred volumes. He tried all the drawers here too. Where would he hide a key? Hanging behind the door was a grey, suit jacket. He sank his hand in one pocket after another. In the inside, right-hand, he found a small key which looked likely. The door slid easily. He was in the garden which stretched away on either side and descended far ahead. He went quickly forward. There was no sign of anyone. Was it a trap? Were they watching him and laughing? What if they were? A trickster was always in danger of being tricked. The lawn sloped steeply. He began to jog keeping his eyes open for any opportunity. He passed an old apple tree whose branches hadn't been lopped for years and hung low and heavy. As he slowed to observe, he noticed two compost bins by the hedge. He went to investigate. Half a dozen rats scurried from between the black, plastic containers, one running over his shoes. The bins were about a metre and a half high. If he stood atop, his head would be above the hedge. Branches from the silver birch in the next garden spread high. The difficulty was to balance on the rim. The container was full of soggy grass cuttings, to put his weight on them was to risk sinking. He hoisted himself so his knees were on the edge, pulled his right leg up and tried to stand but overbalanced and tumbled onto the lawn. Perhaps the best was to try backwards, push off with his feet, his hands on the plastic, get his backside in place and then leaning over to the bin to his left get both feet established, grab the hedge and the branches to raise himself. With great effort he managed it, pulled himself up on a sturdy silver branch, swung his belly over it and clambered till he was over the hedge, standing on the branch, two and half metres from the ground. A dog began to bark, deeply and loud. It appeared at the roots, a Rottweiler, thick-necked, heavy, mature and intent.

"Hello there, boy. Okay boy. Whoa, whoa, calm down, boy, calm down."

He'd never had any nervousness of dogs, his family always having had a pet, and often a big dog. He was used to other animals rearing and growling when he walked the Alsatian or the Dobermann. Guarding its territory, the animal was jumping at the trunk, its front paws scratching at the bark. In spite of his confidence, it would be foolish to climb down. The beast was doing its job. It would get its teeth in his leg or arm, or maybe even his neck. He had no chance of fighting off an eleven stone, angry sentry. Nor of calming it with friendly tones.

"Eric !" a child's voice called.

A girl of ten or so came into view. She slid her fingers into the dog's collar as she looked up at X.

"Hello," he said. "Sorry to have upset your dog, only…"

What was he to say? That he was trying to escape? No doubt she was as controlled as the others. Probably she'd run for an adult or call the police.

"I know it looks odd, but I'm locked in. I can't get out of the front of the house, you see. So I was trying to find a way. That's why I ended up here."

The girl was patting the dog and telling it to be quiet. She looked up and squinted at him. She had auburn hair and freckles across her nose and wore a charming, blue, cotton dress with a flared skirt and sandals. Her arms and legs were tanned. She was just a kid. Surely there was innocence in this place.

"Maybe you could put the dog away and I could climb down. That's if you don't mind me being in your garden. If you do, I'll climb back over."

"The dog won't bite," she said. "Eric, be quiet now."

"I think it'd be best if you put the dog indoors."

"He won't bite."

X wondered if he should go back, but this was a chance of escape. If the dog left him alone perhaps he could find out from the child where he was and how to get away.

"Okay. I'll swing down. Stand clear. I don't want to alarm Eric."

The girl stepped back a few paces.

"Be quiet, Eric. Good boy."

She pulled the animal close to her as X reasoned she wouldn't have the strength to hold it back if it decided to come for him, and swinging down from a tree into its territory was likely to incite its defensive instincts. He hooked his belly over the branch, gripped it and let himself go, dropping the sixty centimetres to the ground. The dog barked roughly and wildly, straining against the child's hold. She wrapped her left arm around its neck and struggled.

"Okay, Eric," said X. "Good dog, good boy," but the emollient tone made no difference.

"Stay there," said the girl.

She pulled on the collar with both hands.

"Come on, Eric. This way. Come on. Stop it, Eric."

On the patio was a short chain fixed to a concrete post. She attached the beast, went inside, and returned with a muzzle which she fitted with difficulty.

"He's safe now," she said, standing on the edge of the lawn.

"Thanks. Look, I'm sorry to invade your privacy, but do you think I could go through your house. I was locked in, you see."

The girl looked at him quizzically, turned her head to the house and looked back.

"I don't know."

"Are your parents at home?"

"No."

"Are you alone?"

"No, I'm with Eric."

"Of course. If I could just nip out of your front door. It'll take a few seconds, that's all."

"Who are you?" she said.

"I'm just a bloke," he said, and laughed. "I lost my way. I was watching the tennis. I don't know how I ended up next door. Whose house is it?"

"I don't know."

"Don't you have neighbours?"

"Sometimes."

"I see. What's your name?"

"I'm not telling."

"No, that's very sensible. Anyway, what do you think? Can I go through your house."

She examined him for a few seconds, skipped across the patio, into the house emerging with a weapon in her hands. X was unfamiliar with guns, but it was the kind of automatic seen in the hands of soldiers in films and on tv. In the hands of a small, sweet girl it looked preposterous.

"Is that yours?"

"It's for protection."

"Yes, but I'm no threat," he said, raising his palms.

"You can go into the house if you want."

"Okay. Okay. No need to point that thing at me."

He circumnavigated the dog which strained at the chain and growled.. The kitchen was wide. At its centre was a large island and round the edges, cupboards with glossy, grey doors. A tall, steel fridge, a washing machine, a spin dryer stood against the facing wall.

"Sit down," she said.

"Right, thanks."

He sat on one of the high-backed chairs at the long table.

"This is a very nice place. Your parents are doing well."

"I don't live with my parents."

"Oh, sorry. Well, whoever you live with."

"Are you a criminal?"

"No," he said with a laugh. "I came for an interview. For a job. Some time ago. Not here. As I matter of fact, I don't know where I am. Where is this place?"

"Elephia."

"Ah, that's the country?"

"I don't know. It's where we live."

"Right, maybe the town."

"Yes."

"As I said, I was watching the tennis. The big tournament. It must be nearby."

"I don't know."

"An arena. Huge place. Is there something like that here?"

She shook her head.

"Anyway, I'm not a criminal. I've just got caught up in some kind of mistake. I shouldn't be here, you see. I need to get back to where I come from."

A mobile chimed. The child turned to look for it and for an instant he contemplated overpowering her; but she was a child. Gun or otherwise, she was young and vulnerable and he was a grown man. She picked up the phone from the work surface.

"No. Eric is with me. Yes. There's a man here. I don't know. Yes. I've got the gun. The one from the kitchen. No. He's sitting here. I don't know. He wants to leave. By the garden. Yes. From the tree. No. Okay. Eric is here. Okay."

She laid the gun on the surface.

"She says I have to let you go."

"Who does?"

"The woman on the phone."

"Does she look after you?"

"No."

"Do you know who she is?"

"Yes."

"Is she part of your family?"

"No, she comes here sometimes, and she rings."

"I see. Well, is it all right if I leave now."

"If you want. I can show you my dolls."

"Dolls. Do you have lots?"

"Come and see."

She skipped along the hallway and up the stairs where he followed her to her neat, girly bedroom. On the wall was a poster of the four he'd seen perform. Over her little desk was the adage: "My brain works best when I'm daydreaming." Four long shelves were occupied by dolls of many nationalities. She stood on the bed and began to take them down and hand them to him.

"This one is from Iceland."

"Iceland? Have you been there?"

"No. People bring them back for me."

"Your family?"

"Many people."

"That's nice of them. You must have been collecting for a long time."

"Since I was a little girl. This is from Indonesia."

"Wow. That's a long way from Iceland."

"This is one of my favourites, it's from Senegal."

"Do you know where Senegal is?"

"Yes."

"Are we near there?"

"I don't know."

She charmed a swift hour in explaining her collection and setting all the dolls back in their rightful place.

"Well, thanks. That was really good. It's an amazing collection. But I think I'd better be going now."

"Are you hungry?"

"Hungry? Maybe a bit peckish."

"There's food in the fridge. They leave it for me."

Cooked meats, salads, coleslaw, pasta, cheeses, sandwiches, chicken breasts and wings, olives, cooked sausages, pickles, beetroot: she took plates and dishes out one by one and set them on the table.

"There's enough here for ten !" he said. "They must've been expecting a crowd."

"I might be on my own a few days. Or with Eric."

"Is that okay?"

"I don't mind."

"Do your friends come round?"

"If they're allowed."

"Yes, there are always adults stopping you doing what you want aren't there."

He ate and the child ate opposite him. At length, she dropped from her stool, took a can of drink from the fridge, switched on the coffee machine and brought him a filled cup, a little jug of milk and a bowl of sugar.

"How did you know I like coffee?"

"Adults do."

When he was sated, he cleared up and stashed the remains in the fridge.

"We could watch a film," she said.

"We could."

He sat beside her on the sofa as she searched the channels, landed on cartoon and looked up at him:

"This is good."

"Okay."

"Have you seen it before?"

"No."

"It's really funny."

"Good, I like a laugh."

"The outsiders get chased away by the animals."

"Ah. The outsiders are bad, are they."

"Very."

"What do they do?"

"I don't know. They're just bad people."

"All of them?"

She nodded. He watched the animation for a few seconds.

"You wouldn't expect them all to be bad, would you?"

"Why not?"

"Well, people aren't usually bad or good, are they. They make some good choices and some bad ones."

"No, the outsiders are always bad."

A sly-looking character was sneaking round a fence. A horde of ants came hurrying, infested his clothes and he ran away scratching a screaming.

"Serve him right," said the girl.

"Poor bloke."

"He should stay where he belongs."

The story unfolded in a series of attempts by various malicious-seeming outsiders to gain access, always to be chased away set upon or devoured by fearsomely protective beasts. The child was delighted.

"Look at that, he bit his head off."

"Yeah, that's quite a mouth."

She leant against him as she watched and while he was glad she trusted him he was disturbed by a growing dislike. She was a child. It wasn't her fault if the television spread a hateful message, yet he couldn't prevent himself feeling negatively. He almost wanted to upbraid her. It would be cruel. Maybe he could gently suggest the outsiders might have some good points, or a reason to seek admittance, but the entertainment was carefully structured to direct the child's emotions. Disdain of the outsider was requisite.

Her head began to nod and eventually she fell asleep against his shoulder. He flicked the channel and landed on a news broadcast. The main item was about the testing of a new weapon, said to inflict devastating damage on the enemy without warning. The latter was the great new development. Previous arms had been detectable and their launching impossible without the enemy having some anticipation, but this permitted strikes in seconds. It would guarantee decimation before any chance of retaliation.

Night had fallen. He lifted the child and carried her to her bed, went out onto the patio and at once the dog strained at the chain and began its from-the-depths growl. Stepping back inside he wondered if he should bring the dog in too. It was muzzled. Yet it could still leap at him and its size and strength would poleaxe him. Leaving it outside overnight seemed cruel, but he didn't dare try the alternative.

The darkness could be his friend. He could make the house secure and leave, stick to quiet routes, walk till morning and be miles away. Or maybe he could find a bike or even steal a car. The idea, troubled him. He didn't want to be a thief. His situation might be desperate, but he didn't want to abandon his values. He went upstairs and checked on the girl who was sleeping peacefully. Could he leave her on her own? Maybe he could get the dog up here and lock him in her room. Even unable to bite he was an impressive guard; but to leave the girl seemed irresponsible. Though he had no connection to her, no responsibility for her in any conventional sense, he was here. He was an adult. She had fallen asleep against him like any child who wants reassurance. Supposing she woke in the night. Suppose an intruder. He could leave early. Dawn. He could take her breakfast and tell her he had to go, ensure she had adults she could contact. He took a beer from the fridge, sat once more on the sofa and searched for an interesting programme. There was a woman, very shapely and alluring in a tight, silver dress, low cut front and back, singing. A lovely mezzo-soprano, she performed ballads, up-tempo numbers, swayed her hips, clicked her fingers and avoided looking at the camera. He was charmed. When he locked the doors and took himself off to bed he was relaxed and yawning as if in his own house; as if everything was normal and tomorrow would be another working day.

A noise downstairs woke him. The sun was already bright, a thin shaft of light from the edge of the curtains hitting the floor to his left. His calm ebbed quickly and anxious thoughts of the girl, the dog, his own safety began to filter. He'd slept naked and wondered if he should pull on his clothes or duck under the shower. He took the towel hanging behind the door, wrapped it round his waist and went to see the child. Her bed was empty. He tried the other rooms, went down to the kitchen where the patio doors were wide open. Eric was sniffing the lawn. He froze a second, thinking he would have to take refuge upstairs, but the dog turned its head and galloped towards him barking thunderously. He looked for an exit, saw the gun on the work surface, grabbed it, aimed, squeezed the trigger, recoiled from the power as the animal collapsed on the floor its blood spreading, warm and thick.

He dressed in a panic, left by the front door, turned left along a quiet road bordered by big houses with extensive gardens and finding a set of concrete steps which dipped down through a wood, took them in pairs arriving breathless at the base on a path of black, compacted earth. To his right there seemed to be a break in the trees, more light, suggesting some kind of settlement or perhaps another quiet road. He headed left where the path grew narrower, the wood thicker, the undergrowth more fulsome. The way twisted. He climbed over fallen trunks, leapt deep puddles, squelched through patches of mud arriving at a river at the far side of which was a town. He paused to survey the tall buildings: a spire, several towers. How far was it? Maybe a mile. Perhaps he would have a chance there. To the right was a bridge, traffic rising and falling, coming and going. He turned left and followed the higgeldy-piggeldy path which narrowed after a mile, the bushes at either side having to be brushed away to pass. At one point, his progress was blocked by mud and water through which horses had trodden. He was forced to bend back branches, double himself and shuffle through the undergrowth. An iron kissing-gate led to an open area of grass where sheep were grazing. Ahead were two pylons whose buzzing he heard as he passed beneath. The river widened, meandered, until, at some five miles or so, he came to wide marshes. Sheep were in large numbers, but there was no sign of a farm. Another mile and he heard gunshots. He paused. Would he be shot as an intruder? Was this a land where a stranger was to be suspected and shooting came before questions? He was too tired to walk back, it was impossible to lie down here and spend the night. He advanced cautiously. A building came into view, perhaps a barn, then an obvious farmhouse. Immediately he began to think of food and drink. An object flew into the sky, an echoing explosion followed and the disc was shattered. He walked towards the house and in time saw a woman alone. loading the clay pigeons, lifting the gun, triggering release, pushing the stock against her shoulder and blasting. When she noticed him, she broke the barrel, inserted two cartridges, closed it and pointed at him.

"Hello," he called. "Sorry, I'm a bit lost. I'm not trespassing am I ?"

She stood still, the gun at her hip. He continued steadily, his palms held up.

"Sorry. Sorry. I've gone astray, a bit."

"Where are you trying to get to?"

"I don't know. I mean, I'm not quite sure where I went wrong. Where is this?"

"The marshes."

"Yes. Pleased to meet you?"

He offered his hand but she looked him steadily in the eyes.

"Nobody comes walking this way."

"I see. It's very pretty. The river and so on. Is there anywhere I could get something to drink? A pub?"

She let the barrel point to the ground, turned and twitched her head to indicate he should follow. They skirted the house, came to a lane where, a hundred, metres further on was a tiny bar, its weather-beaten sign over the door: *The Night Heron* . She unlocked, Inside was one room big enough for half a dozen, a two metre bar with one pump. She pulled him a dark pint.

"I don't suppose you serve food?"

"What would you like?" she said without lifting her eyes.

"Anything. Even a bag of crisps would be a feast. I'm ravenous."

She looked up, set the glass on a beer mat.

"Soup?"

"Oh yes, that would be great."

"Sit down."

He obeyed: his legs were aching. She pulled aside a dark blue curtain and went into the rear space. The rest and the beer were luxurious. He didn't know where he was. He had no idea what was going to happen to him. No doubt his minder would be after him. Why hadn't she caught up with him already? Was it a game? If only he could find out where he was. He ought to be able to tell from the flora and fauna, but he'd encountered no wild animals and none of the birds had looked exotic. It was warm ,but not greatly more than home in summer. Though the woman had pointed her shotgun at him, he felt drawn to her. Not in any erotic way, but as a companion. She was offering him food. He recalled the recent meals he'd been treated to. Was this woman being generous or was she manipulating him? His exhaustion got the better of him. He was going to enjoy her company and her food. Maybe he could stay here. Perhaps he would be safe. Or maybe she'd help him escape.

The grey bowl sat in the middle of a big, white plate, accompanied by a chunk of granary bread and a knob of butter. She set it on the little square table.

"Thanks, that's terrific."

She disappeared again and returned with two triangle sandwiches, thick cut bread and a handsome portion of beef between the slices, a salad alongside, green leaves, onion, tomato.

"Another pint?"

"I wouldn't mind."

While he ate, she busied herself behind the bar with little tasks of cleaning and storing, going through the curtain now and again and returning to set to work again. He wondered if she was simply keeping an eye on him. When he'd finished the meal and drunk half his second pint he said:

"Do you run this place on your own?"

Her dark eyes flashed at him. She was a sultry-skinned woman with thick black hair. Perhaps Iberian. Was that where he was? But people moved around the globe so much.

"I keep myself to myself."

"Well, you make a good soup and a delicious sandwich. I should think your customers are delighted."

"Coffee?"

"I wouldn't mind a tea, if that's okay."

She nodded.

"Let's go to the house."

In the living-room, a log fire was burning in the hearth despite the warmth. There were two long sofas each at right angles to the chimney. A sheepdog was lying on the blue rug and barely stirred as they entered. Everything was clean and tidy. On the mantlepiece were framed pictures: a bride and groom, an old woman, a boy of four or five. She brought a pot, two cups and saucers, a little China jug of milk and sugar bowl and a plate with thick slices of fruit cake.

"This is a nice room."

"I like it."

"Do you live alone."

"No, my son will be home soon."

"Ah, how old is he?"

"Seventeen."

"Student?"

"No."

"Just the two of you, then?"

"That's right."

"You've certainly got plenty of room."

She poured.

"They'll be coming for you soon?"

"What?"

"I have to look after you in the meantime."

"You are looking after me, but who is coming for me and how do you know?"

"I got a message."

"Who from?"

She shrugged.

"The ones who make the decisions."

"Don't you know who they are?"

"How would it help me?"

"You should know. If a decision affects you, you should have a say."

"I don't want a say."

"Don't you?"

"No, I want them to make the right decisions for me."

"The machine decides?"

"Yes."

"Who controls the machine?"

"They do, I suppose."

He drank his tea, which was exactly as he liked it. His minder was on the way. If he made a run for it now, would the woman grab the shotgun? She'd been instructed to look after him. If her obedience was as complete as it appeared he would be safe.

"Would it make any difference to you if I was to escape?"

"How?"

"You could help me. Which way can I go that'll make it difficult for them to find me?"

"They'll find you anywhere."

"I want to get back to where I came from. You see, I was called for an interview…"

"So was I."

"When?"

"Years ago. Before my son was born."

"What happened?"

"They looked after me. I had a good time. I had everything I wanted. I was with the important people. Then my son was born and they gave me this place when he was about five and we've been here since."

"Did you never want to escape?"

"I can't remember. Maybe at first, but I had such lovely things. A flat, a car, clothes, entertainment. Life was a party."

"Where were you before you came here?"

"We don't talk about that."

"Wouldn't you like to?"

"Not allowed. The outsiders."

"You were an outsider once."

"Yes,"

"Maybe there are good things about being an outsider."

"No. They're a threat."

"Were you a threat?"

"I must've been."

"Am I?"

"You won't be."

"How can you be so sure?"

"Time will change you. It happens quickly."

"They've looked after me too, but I don't like it. I want to make my own choices. I'm going before they get here. Which is the best way?"

"It makes no difference."

"Shall I head for the town? Could I lie low there?"

"How would you do that?"

"I don't know. Find a place to stay. Keep in the shadows. There must be things going on they don't know about."

She shook her head.

"Will you help me?" he said.

"I'll look after you."

"By helping me escape?"

"No, by giving you what you need."

"What I need is to escape."

"That's not what they mean. I can be as nice to you as you like."

He wanted to ask her if he could take the gun, but would he have the nerve to use it? No. He wouldn't shoot the minder, but to brandish it might deter her.

"I don't suppose there's any point asking you to say I haven't been here."

"They know."

"I'm going now. Don't watch me then you won't have to say which way I went."

She shrugged.

"Thanks for the food, it was lovely."

"You should stay. You'll be looked after."

He ran back to the little bar, veered left, vaulted a gate into a field of cows and jogged over the uneven ground. In the distance was a wood which curved to the right. They'd know he was there, but the trees and bushes must offer some cover. Once amongst them he felt relieved, slowed and stepped along the path. Many feet must have walked here. It must lead somewhere. Perhaps it would be best to cut off into the trees and shrubs, make his own path through the undergrowth; but the idea that they knew where he was whatever he did fuddled his thinking. Where was he? Perhaps not so far from home as he imagined. After all, the interview venue was in his home town. How had they established themselves there? What kind of enterprise were they apparently running? It struck him he had no idea. Had they made it clear or even mentioned it? He couldn't recall having any inkling of the nature of their undertaking. Why had he turned up for an interview without knowing? It was the invitation which had flattered him and made him less vigilant than he should have been. He realised he'd gone along in a mood of self-regarding willingness. They wanted him, though he had no idea who they were or how they knew him. Who wouldn't be self-complaisant if some outside agency appeared to offer blandishments? He had been picked out. He was called upon. It had shut down the self-critical or even sensibly cautious part of his mind. Yet, if they had an operation in his town, perhaps they were in all places. Maybe they were surreptitiously inserting themselves in all institutions. How could he work out if he was much closer to home than he realised? He stopped and looked at the vegetation. There was nothing unfamiliar. In the gaps between the rhododendrons, huge nettles grew. Nettles ! He'd stung himself several times as a kid trying to prove to his mates he could grasp one and be unscathed.

This might be a wood he'd played in as a child. Maybe there was a stream and a rope swing. Perhaps the abandoned farmhouse was on the far edge. Was his house no more than a few miles away? How far had he walked when he escaped from the interview venue? Then the car ride and after, the helicopter. Was that enough for him to be a long distance from home? He found it impossible to conceive of the length of time he'd been travelling.

He pressed on till dark. Surely he was safe now, at least for a while. The chill of night began to close in. He pulled up grasses, tore off slender branches, crawled inside a big bush and formed a makeshift bed. He was going to be cold but at least he'd been fed. Hunger wouldn't trouble him for a few hours. Maybe he should have stayed with the woman. Perhaps she'd have given him a bed. He could have left in the morning after a good breakfast. No doubt she had eggs, bacon, sausages, mushrooms, tomatoes and thick slices of that lovely bread toasted. Yes, it would have been wonderful, but not as wonderful as the idea of being free.

He was woken by noise and a touch.

"It's me."

The minder shone a torch on his face.

"Christ."

"Wrap this round you. You'll be hypothermic."

She pulled a survival blanket across his shoulders.

"Come on, it's not too far to my car. Can you walk?"

"Of course I can walk. I've just got cold hands and feet."

"What's the point of sleeping in a bush when a lovely bed and warm room are offered?"

"The terms of the offer don't suit me."

Why didn't he refuse to go with her? What would she do? He was stronger. She couldn't force him, unless she carried a weapon; but the scene in the restaurant came back to him. If he rebelled would goons appear out of nowhere, bind him hand and foot and carry him to who knows where? Better to cooperate given she would offer him comfort. A warm shower, a sleep on a firm mattress. Was he being seduced into conformity? No, he would find another way to escape.

She went ahead shining her beam, following the path by which he'd arrived. Her car was parked outside the farmhouse where an upstairs light was burning. It was a relief to be installed on the heated passenger seat. She sped along the deserted lanes. Here and there he believed he recognised something. A large, modern house set in its own acre, distant from the road as they turned sharply right, looked vaguely like a place he'd been invited to for a party.

"I think I've been here before," he said.

"No, you haven't."

"How do you know?"

"You've never been anywhere near here. This is closed territory to outsiders"

"What about the girl?"

"What girl?"

"The girl with the dog. Eric. What happened to her?"

"Don't know anything about her."

She was lying. If they could find him hidden under a bush two miles into a wood, in the middle of the night, they knew he'd spent the night in the girl's house. Why did they want to deny it? Simply to confuse him? If he was off his stride he might be more likely to give in.

"Are we going to see the rest of the tennis tournament?" he said.

"Would you like to?"

"Not particularly."

"It's a marvellous spectacle though, isn't it?"

"In its way."

"Oh, they do it brilliantly. The crowds love it. Then there's television and online. Hundreds of millions are riveted."

Hundreds of millions? He was puzzled. She talked as if their regime was global, but surely they were some smallish sect.

"That must be worldwide."

"Of course."

"How do you connect to people all over the globe?"

"It's the simplest thing. People have devices. You bounce a signal off a satellite."

"Yes, but most of the world must be outsiders to you."

"Only in a certain sense."

"What sense?"

"Did the woman in the farmhouse look after you?"

"She fed me."

"That's a start."

They were driving through a suburb, big houses on either side , tall hedges, a little row of shops, a pub.

"Nice place," he said.

"Isn't it. Pity we can't stop."

"We could have a stroll."

"In the middle of the night? We'd get picked up by the police."

What did she have to fear from the police?

"They'd have no power over you, would they?"

"The law is the law."

"What does the law say about holding people against their will?"

"Not permitted."

Turning off the main road they slowed. They were now on an avenue where modest semis faced enormous, million-pound places, one with a thatched roof. They glided at twenty past the cheaper places and came to what at first seemed to be a hotel. Electronic gates opened onto a wide driveway. They pulled up in front of a vast edifice dominated by stone bay windows at both levels. The dark blue double doors opened. Floodlights illuminated the area. He followed her into an extensive, square hallway,

"Like it?"

"Very nice."

"You can take that off now," she said, gently removing the survival blanket.

A butler emerged with a tray carrying a teapot, a cup and saucer, milk and sugar, a glass and a bottle of beer.

"Would you like this in the lounge, sir, or your room?"

"I think I'll go to my room."

"Very good, sir."

She followed them up the wide stairs, along a landing onto which gave half a dozen doors and into a warm room whose king size's headboard was against the chimney breast. X stood and surveyed for a moment.

"You never spare any expense, do you?"

"We want you to be comfortable."

"I know."

"Thank you," she said to the butler, who placed the tray on the bedside table and left.

"A shower will warm and freshen you up."

"No, thanks. I'll have the tea and get to sleep."

"There's room for both of us."

He feared she would impose herself. What could he do if she stripped off and got into bed?

"I'd much prefer to be on my own."

"Are you sure?"

"Certain."

"Sooner or later you'll want comfort."

"I can look after myself."

"Shall I have breakfast brought up here?"

"That'll be fine."

"Do you like sailing?"

"Sailing?"

"There's a yacht booked for tomorrow. The weather is set to be glorious. We'll go out to sea for a few days."

The idea brought sudden depression. No doubt there would be luxury and plentiful food and drink; no doubt also entertainment of all kinds; but what chance would he have of any kind of escape once they were on the open sea?

"I look forward to it," he said.

Was there any point checking the windows? Could he sneak out, down the stairs, through the front door and make a run for it? Or maybe find the keys to her car? He was too tired. The tea, brewed to perfection warmed him. He stripped off, doused his face in warm water in the en suite, cleaned his teeth with the electric brush and got between the pristine sheets. The warmth was lovely. Sleep was gaining on him but he was trying to keep his mind on how to extricate himself. There must be some flaw. Tomorrow. When he woke. Tomorrow he would think hard.

He was lying with his hands behind his head reflecting that he'd never had to think through his actions so seriously. His life had moved on, as if pre-determined, but looking back he was aware his choices had been decisive. Nothing moves on of its own accord, he concluded, but immediately found himself questioning his certainty. He was here because he'd made a choice. It was open to him not to accept the bizarre invitation. Had he done so, he would have no knowledge of the world he was now part of. We can always choose but we do so with little or no idea of what our choices will lead to. The essential was principle. What principle had made him attend the interview? Perhaps it was absence of principle.

Was it pure opportunism? Was it mere expediency? Or conformism? An invitation arrived, he needed a job, he complied but without thinking through properly what he was doing. Who had he mentioned the interview to? His mother. M. A friend or two. He couldn't remember. He'd been too lackadaisical. Drift. Let things happen. Go with the flow. He hated the expression. What was "the flow"? Stupid. He was criticising himself for his inadvertence when the door opened and a girl of about eighteen entered.

"Do you want your shower or your breakfast first?"

She was a charming, slender, blonde lass, very appealing, the kind of girl he might have developed a longing for, telephoned, messaged, been willing to put up with a lot for, but now he dreaded the thought of the shower.

"Breakfast, please."

"Okay. It's ready for you. I'll bring it up."

"Thanks a lot."

While she was away, he could get dressed, but he needed a shave and a wash. He would accept the food, jump out of bed when she'd gone, shower and shave quickly, pull on his clothes and be eating when she returned.

She set the tray over his legs, as if he was a hospital patient, unable to get to his feet. The array was exactly what he would have requested. For an instant, he wondered if he should complain, claim it wasn't to his taste; but no doubt they'd spot the deception.

"Lovely. Thank you."

"I'll run the shower while you're eating so it'll be nice and warm."

"No, no. It'll be fine. Really. I'd rather be left alone to eat, if you don't mind."

"I'm not allowed to do that."

"Make your own choice."

She stopped in the little task of tidying she'd begun.

"I can't do that?"

"Why not?"

"I don't decide."

"Who does?"

She resumed rearranging the items on the surface before the mirror.

"I don't know. Those who know best."

"Would you like some toast?" he said, raising himself a little.

"No, thanks."

"It's delicious."

"No, it's okay."

"The thing is, I want my privacy."

"It's private in here."

"Not if you get in the shower with me."

"No one will see us."

"No, but I like to choose who I shower with."

"I'm required to give you a shower."

"Try not doing what you're required to do."

"Things will go wrong if I do that."

"How do you know?"

"Everything works well if we do what we're told."

"That's what you're told."

"Anyway, I have to do what I'm instructed. That keeps things simple."

"Doesn't it feel wrong?"

"No."

"It must do. Don't you ever want to do something other than you're required to?"

"Of course, but we're trained not to."

"Try it, just once and see how it feels."

"What would be the point?"

"You'd know how it feels. You might find it beneficial."

"But I'd be in trouble."

"What kind of trouble?"

"I don't know."

"Will this conversation get you in trouble?"

"Not if do what I'm supposed to."

"You're doing what you're supposed to. I'm the one objecting. When I've finished this, which, by the way, is just as I like it, I'm going to shave and shower on my own. I'm not going to let you come near me."

"I don't understand that."

"It's simple. I insist on choosing."

"Why would you choose to turn down something nice?"

"Because having something nice forced on you is unpleasant."

She stiffened and stared.

"I'm very good at it."

"Oh, I'm sure. I'm not criticising you or suggesting you wouldn't be attentive. But can't you see that saying no to something apparently pleasurable can be more important than giving in?"

"No."

"You can stay in this room. You've done what you're supposed to do. I'm the one who's prevented you."

"I still might be in trouble."

He recalled the restaurant incident and worried she might be subject to violence. Wouldn't it be better to go along with things to prevent that? Yet that was to grant power to whoever made the decisions, to relinquish forever the possibility of choice. If they could always threaten punishment, violence, hand-ties, incarceration, there was no freedom. It had to be possible to choose without fear. He knew that wasn't possible. He did fear for her. She was a delightful young girl who ought to be enjoying life, finding her way; she ought not to have the threat of violence nestling in her viscera and preventing her from being what she chose. He had to choose in spite of fear. Was that courageous? Not if the punishment wouldn't fall on him. Perhaps it was even cowardly. Was the brave thing to put up with the discomfort of the assisted shower? He was in an impossible situation, which was what they required.

"You're afraid of what they might do to you."

"Of course."

"I'm afraid of it too."

He set down his cup and surveyed the ceiling, the walls, the floor.

"However you're seeing and hearing this, understand this young woman has done exactly as you asked, but if she comes into the bathroom with me I shall inflict harm on her. If anyone is to blame, it's me. If anyone is to be punished, it's me. She is innocent. I won't let her come near me in the shower. I'm asserting my right to be left alone if I wish."

He lifted the tray and signalled to her to remove it. She took it and set it by the door.

"You can go now."

She shook her head. He got out of bed hiding himself with his t-shirt and went into the bathroom. Before the mirror he debated between the electric and wet shave, decided on the latter and squirted the foam into his palm. She came through the door and stood behind him, resting her hands on his waist. He turned to face her.

"Didn't you hear what I said?"

"You won't hurt me."

"How do you know?"

"I can tell."

He pushed her gently away, opened the door, directed her to the bed, sat her on the edge and stepped back.

"Stay there."

She didn't interrupt as he took a shower. When he returned, a towel round his waist, she was in tears. Wasn't it possible to extricate himself without causing distress? For a second, he wished he'd allowed her to do what she was ordered. Was it so bad for him? Couldn't he have rationalised it by telling himself he was doing it for her sake? Try as he might, it remained true that making the choice was the crucial matter.

"You must be familiar with the place," he said, aware it was absurd to speak openly when he was being spied on, "is there a way I could escape?"

She shook her head as she sobbed.

"You could come with me."

"I don't want to. Why should I leave?"

"Because away from here you can choose how to act."

"I might choose badly."

"Yes, with a bit of luck."

"I don't understand that."

"No, they've made sure you don't."

She got up swiftly and left before he could remonstrate. He was slightly sickened by the thought she might suffer but he'd taken an important step. Henceforth, he would do everything he could to deny what they sought to make him accept.

Feeling emboldened, he decided to head down the stairs, out of the front door and away in whatever direction seemed best, but before he was out of the room his minder was at the door.

"Your yacht awaits you."

"I'm not going."

"Don't be silly, everyone's waiting."

"I'm serious. You'll have to drag me there."

"No, I won't. Come on."

"I warn you, I'll put up a fight. Even if the goons like those in the restaurant arrive."

"There'll be no fighting."

"I'm staying here."

She walked calmly over to him, smiled, took his arm and guided him, like a reluctant child being coaxed into school for the first time. He could have shaken her off, hit her, grabbed her and overpowered her. He was four inches taller and much stronger; but he blenched from force. He had no fear she might retaliate or that heavies would come running and beat him up. He would almost have preferred to take a beating than to go willingly onto the boat. What he was incapable of was hurting her. Was that cowardice or some form of misplaced chivalry?

He was in the passenger seat and she gunned away from the house, the tyres giving a little screech. The yacht was berthed in a marina which looked remotely familiar. A converted dock which had once welcomed ships from around the world, it had once been a busy, commercial arena, but was now a calm, leisure facility. The capstans, still in place, had been painted shiny black. There were little boats, bobbing at the far end, where people sat on the terrace of a café, next to a chandler's. The yacht was moored more centrally, huge, white, its mast towering, moving heavily in the gently rocking water. A man in white nauticals walked from bow to stern. There were a dozen milling on the quay.

"Let's get on board."

"I'll give it a miss, if you don't mind."

"You don't know what's good for you," she said, took his hand and pulled him up the gangway. She led him aft, and they sat by the swimming pool.

"Doesn't it look inviting?"

"I haven't brought my trunks."

"Easily solved. Do you like swimming?"

"No, I can't even doggy paddle."

As a teenager he swam for his county. Crawl was his forte but he competed in the medley relay. His father had been keen, recklessly swimming in reservoirs and diving into chilly lakes. X had learnt early and coaxed by his dad was confident in the water as a toddler. Swimming had been more or less effortless, but his facility recognised, he was grabbed by teams and trained to the point of exhaustion. At eighteen he decided he wanted to swim for pleasure and to disappointment and groans, gave up competition.

"That's not our understanding."

"What is your understanding?"

"You've got quite a horde of cups and medals."

"For swimming?"

"Yes."

"No, you've got your wires crossed. I tell you, I can't stay afloat."

The folk from the quay boarded, the gangway was lifted and the boat began its graceful, slow turn, churning the water at its stern. The siren sounded for the swing bridge, the traffic stopped at either end and like a swan whose underwater effort is invisible, the weighty boat glided out of the estuary and onto the open water. X leaned over the starboard rail surveying the water, as if by studying it he might work out which ocean it might be. When she joined him he said:

"The Pacific."

"What?"

"I can tell by looking at it. The oceans of the world move in slightly different ways."

"Come on, there's coffee downstairs and then music you'll enjoy."

"A brass band?"

"Much better than that."

"Nothing is better than a brass band."

Below deck a small room had been set up for a gig: a drum kit, electric piano, bass guitar and tenor saxophone awaited their musicians. Chairs with gold legs upholstered in burgundy were set in semi-circular rows. Behind them a waiter in smart black and white was serving coffee and an array of cakes from a table draped in a crisp, red cloth.

"Two, please,"she said.

"Decaffeinated for me," said X.

"Of course, sir."

X had hoped the request would be refused, but the waiter disappeared for thirty seconds, came back with a pot of swaying dark liquid and poured.

"Milk and sugar are on the end there, sir."

"Carrot cake? she said.

"Watching my waistline."

They sat on the front row, close to the piano. He felt his heart pounding and was aware of his mental conflict. The event augured well, the instruments reminding him of many gigs. Though so early in the day was curious for jazz, after nine in the evening being more appropriate, he couldn't help anticipating positively; yet at the same time that they knew his fondness maddened him. No doubt they knew too of his dad's record collection. He wanted not to enjoy, but the only possibility was that the musicians were incompetent amateurs. A neat, smallish woman of about thirty-five stepped confidently over the wires, sat at the drums and played a few subdued rolls. The bass was gathered by a tall, angular man with long, dark hair, probably first sported in the late sixties. To the piano arrived a thin bloke wearing a pork pie hat and heavy black glasses. He scurried over the keys, chimed a few chord progressions as the sax player, bulky, blonde, dressed in a smart, blue suit, lifted his instrument, hooked it up, fingered a quick run, counted in and began "*Southern Parade*"

"Recognise it?"

The melody was composed by his dad's old friend, a piano player who gigged for decades, supplementing his civil servant's income. One of those highly gifted and accomplished jazzos who have fine reputations in their locale and make the occasional mention at national level, he composed dozens of pieces known to a few. In spite of his discomfort, X couldn't help himself softening to the music. These four were exquisitely talented and remarkably disciplined; it was the latter which permitted the solo flights which, to the unaccustomed ear, could appear as a mere volley of notes. The familiar melodies touched off nostalgia; times when as a kid he sat and listened as his dad tuned into jazz on the radio or put on CDs of Bud Powell, Tony Coe, Chick Corea, Wes Montgomery. He was aware of being seduced. Pandering to his tastes was a subtle way of inveigling him into submission. Yet he saw no reason he shouldn't let himself sink into the pleasure. What else could he do? Jump overboard?

"Excellent, weren't they?" she said when the encore was over. "Would you like me to introduce you?"

"No, thanks."

The boat was far from land. On deck he surveyed the expanse and wondered if the best course was to consign himself to the waves. The idea shocked him. Why should he turn on himself because of what was being done to him? He bore no responsibility. Was that true? Yes, none at all. His negativity should be turned on them. His sense of impotence induced anxiety. He knew what was wrong, what was needed, but had no means to make it happen. How long would he be on this boat? Once he was on dry land, he would do all he could to escape.

He didn' t have to wait as long as he expected, as they docked at an island in the evening. The day had passed watching people swim and compete in deck sports, eating in the fine dining-room- - seven courses over four hours - watching the latest film starring one of the passengers, a handsome, coloured man who spoke impeccable RP. The little port could barely accommodate the long boat. The gangway was lowered, the passengers trotted down to the beach and through a copse to a luxurious huddle of apartments, cafes, restaurants, shops, a little hedonist's paradise.

"We've decided to spend the night here, " she said. "I'll show you your apartment."

He anticipated the perfection which sickened him. He would have preferred a tent and a sleeping bag, a little burner on which to heat water, nipping behind a bush to relieve himself.

When darkness fell the party began. Raucous dance music pumped from speakers, lights were strung across the beach, drinks were served from a bar erected in double-quick time, the anything-goes atmosphere encouraged wild behaviour. A women ten years his senior flung her arms round his neck and bumped her groin against him.

"Oh, you could do me some good," she said, laying her head on his chest.

They made little steps in the sand to the repeated rhythm, a kind of dancing. Her arms were pulling down on him making his back begin to tighten. When she suggested, languorously, they should go to her apartment, he acquiesced.

"Are you on your own?" he said as she flopped onto the bed.

"No, my husband's somewhere. With someone. Don't worry about him."

"Why are you on this boat?"

"Why? To enjoy myself."

She kicked her shoes off roughly, so they flew across the room and hit the wall, at which she laughed like a teenager.

"Yes, but why were you invited?"

"For being a good girl, though right now I'm a naughty one," and she laughed again.

"Do you know all the people here?"

"Some. Some too well, others not well enough."

"And they're all important people, are they?"

"Important? They do what they're required to do. Anyway, why all the questions? Are you with the normalisation force?"

"No, but I've never been to one of these events."

"You must be behaving yourself. Unlike me, ha, ha!"

"Are we private here?"

She rolled over on her stomach.

"We won't be disturbed, if that's what you mean. My husband will be looking for a more tender cut of meat."

"Are we spied on?"

She turned on her side and propped herself on her elbow.

"What kind of question is that? It's the price we pay for hedonism. Who cares? Are you bashful about the machine seeing you naked?"

"Can't we turn it off?"

She fell on her back again and roared.

"You take the biscuit. Come here and get on with it. Can't you see I'm dying for it?"

He went and stood by the bed. She hitched up her dress and pulled off her knickers which she launched like the shoes.

"What is the normalisation force?"

"You know how to make a women feel desired."

"Who runs the machine?"

"It runs itself, dearie."

"We are being observed."

"Observed? How polite? Of course we're being watched and listened to, how else could life go on? Who are you, anyway?"

"Doesn't it bother you?"

"Why should it? I get to ride on this yacht and seduce young men."

"You're choosing to do that."

"Am I? How do you know?"

"Tell me."

"I might if I knew myself."

"Where are we?"

"In the bedroom, sweetie."

"What's the name of this island?"

"What would you like it to be?"

He took hold firmly of her wrists. She resisted a little then her expression darkened.

"You and me are going to leave this island."

She tried to pull her arms free.

"I'm not going to hurt you," he said, "but you're going to help me. You wouldn't be here if you weren't in the know. You're going to help me get free."

"You're crazy."

"Tell me, what island is this? Which ocean is out there? How far is the nearest mainland?"

He heard the door open. His minder was behind him.

"You're missing the party."

"We're having our own," said the woman on the bed.

The minder gathered the shoes and underwear.

"Here, let's get back to the celebration."

"What are we celebrating?" said the other, slipping on her shoes.

"Our good fortune."

The minder stood sentry at the door as the other woman left. X was guided back to the party which disgusted him. He reflected that getting drunk might be the best option, something to obliterate his anguish, but he resisted. He mustn't let himself be overcome. However small, he had to retain an element of resistance. Somehow or other an opportunity would arise.

The following morning, they were back on the boat under clear blue skies and a scorching sun. X wandered the deck looking for a lifeboat. If there had been one, it was just possible he might have been able to get it in the water and himself after it. There were life-jackets and floats. He stood atop the ladder towards the bow. At an opportune moment he could climb down. Buoyed by a jacket and a ring he wouldn't sink, even if some of the bigger waves swept over him. He could kick and stroke away. How far were they now from the island? If he went back there, how would he ever leave it? He looked out over the seemingly endless water. How far could they have travelled? A boat like this might speed along at a fair rate of knots. Maybe they were a hundred miles from the mainland. He couldn't do the calculation. A life-jacket and a ring were silly consolations. In there, he would drown. Of course, they'd pick him up in no time, which would be a greater humiliation than being washed up on the shore, bloated with sea-water.

There was nothing for it but to endure the trip and save his scheming for the return to the mainland.

That afternoon, a helicopter, from which emerged a young woman in a tight, red dress with thick, black, flowing hair, bee-sting lips, curling, long eyelashes, who greeted the waving cheering gaggle with waves, hugs and fulsome expressions of affection and delight, chugged and shimmied onto the deck. X stood by the rail watching and wondering. Later, after their sumptuous meal, she appeared before them, now in a gold dress, a microphone in her hand and, when the wild applause and whooping had died down, explained the game they were going to enjoy. The aim was to deceive those on their table. By convincing them they had no desire to betray them for money, they could win a big money prize. The diners, assisted in their enthusiasm by readily flowing booze, joined in with alacrity and soon there was bitter rivalry behind the loud guffaws. X, forced to participate, engaged minimally.

"Who is this woman?" he said to his minder.

"Our greatest celebrity."

"What made her famous?"

"Being famous. I'll introduce you."

"No, why would she want to meet me?"

"Everybody wants to meet her. You can't turn her down."

"If everybody wants to meet her, how will she have time for me?"

All the same, when the game was over and the winnings had fallen from the ceiling onto the successful table, whose occupants grabbed at it and gathered as if they were starving and it was basic staple, his minder brought the woman to him and she led him onto the dance floor where they were watched avidly by the rest.

"Are you having a good time?" she said.

"Lovely."

"What a wonderful yacht this is. Have you been on it many times?"

"My first."

"Not your last, I'm sure. I've been here dozens of times. Always marvellous."

A Salsa rhythm began to play and she danced expertly, while he floundered.

"Let me show you"

Demonstrating the steps, as if to an idiot, she held his hand and swayed, this way and that.

"Good, good. You see, it's not so difficult."

Around them some of the couples were combining, separating, spinning, pushing one another apart, clinging like leeches. X felt like a non-swimmer in a pool full of champions.

"Maybe I should sit this one out."

"No, no, sweetie. You're doing brilliantly. Follow the steps. You see, one, two, three and, five six seven and…"

The music ended and a great roar of pleasure arose from the little gathering. In response came another rhythm of the same kind and they were under way once more. The dancing went on till the early hours when couples began to drift away till only X and the star, his minder and the drunk from his room were left.

"Bedtime," said the minder and lifted the drunk from her chair.

"So early?"

"Come on. See you in the morning", she said to the other two.

The familiar sense of dread seized X. Was this woman too commanded to see to his needs? Was she genuinely a celebrity or was the whole business a set-up? It seemed absurd that all this might have been laid on for him.

"They tell me you're very famous," he said to her.

"I am, darling."

"Doesn't it get on your nerves?"

She laughed.

"What a curious idea. It brings me lots of money and attention. I get to mix with the best people.."

"Don't you mean the richest?"

"What's the difference, sweetie?"

"Why should you be interested in me? I'm not famous. I have no money."

"Not yet."

"Not ever."

"Don't be so negative," she said in a low voice, leaning towards him, "you never know what might be up ahead."

"Can you summon that helicopter you arrived on?"

"If I want to."

"I'd like to fly. I've never been in a helicopter," he lied.

"Well, we can organise that tomorrow."

"I thought it'd be more exciting in the dark."

"Everything's more exciting in the dark, dear."

"We could fly over the ocean. That would be thrilling."

"Yes, But let's leave it to the morning. When they come for me, I'll take you for a spin."

"In the dark will be more exciting."

"You won't see much."

"That's part of what I fancy. Hovering over the black sea, the waves calling below. I bet the pilot can fly close to the surface."

"What a strange young man you are. I'll see."

She left him. He went up on deck careless of whether she'd be able to find him. The water sploshed against the hull. It was water just like at home. The idea came to him again that he was the victim of some huge hoax; but could everyone be play-acting? His anger impelled him to confront his minder, to demand to be released, but he calmed himself: he had to outwit whatever system it was which had got the better of him. He thought back to the invitation to interview. How had it arrived? E-mail or text? He was at a loss. Why hadn't he registered that? Why at the first disturbing event hadn't he rebelled? He tried to evoke the feeling he'd had when the offer had been made. He'd been thrown by it. He'd wondered how it could be, but he'd gone along with it. Yes, that was it. Going along with it was fatal. Never again. Whatever he objected to, whatever didn't tally with his sentiments, he'd raise his voice, he'd refuse. Why hadn't he? Because everything seemed to be running along nicely, in a way. For him, at least. He'd lost his job and there was unfairness in that. Life was full of annoyances; but they were bumps in the road, not impediments to movement. Now, it all seemed different. He looked back and saw multiple problems. His mother's anxiety, his father's drinking, M's disorientating ambivalence. Why had he never challenged her about it? Why had he never said to his dad he ought to cut down? He went along with things, and now look where he was.

"There you are. I thought you'd gone overboard or found another woman."

"More likely the former than the latter."

"Oh, how flattering. The chopper is coming, if you see what I mean. Though the pilot is grumpy."

It circled, dropped slowly, its tail dipping, rocking left and right till the landing skids touched delicately. They climbed into the cockpit. The pilot gave X a hard stare of accusation.

"Thanks for this," said X. "Never been in one of these."

They soared and tilted, dipped towards the water.

"I told him," she said, "grabbing X's arm, "you wanted a bit of danger."

"Ask him to take us to the mainland."

"Why?"

"I'm tired of the boat. Let's go somewhere busy for a few hours. He can bring us back can't he?"

They flew a few feet above the waves at great speed, then soared again and turned in the black sky. She unfastened herself and spoke to the pilot who shook his head.

"He can't."

"Why not?"

"He's not allowed."

"He's not allowed to do this, is he? But he is."

"We all have our orders, dearie."

"Even you."

"Especially me."

"But you're rich and famous, you can do what you like."

"If I'd done what I like I'd never have been rich and famous."

Should he behave like a desperado, create some crisis as in a cheap film: grab her by the throat and tell the pilot he'd squeeze the life out of her if he didn't fly to the mainland? He had no desire to hurt the woman. She struck him as a victim, a pathetic creature. What if he were to throw himself out? He wouldn't survive long in the black cold, but maybe they'd panic, rescue him and let him go. They must be keeping him for some advantage. If he became a burden they'd release him. Yet how could he be a burden when they pandered to his every need? Maybe he should become whimsical. That wouldn't throw them. They'd simply become more obliging.

"Will he fly us to where I come from?"

"Where's that?"

He told her and she said she'd never heard of it.

"I guess that makes me an outsider," he said.

"Don't be silly, you're one of us. Let's go back."

She clung to his arm all the way and when they were on the quiet deck and the craft had taken off once more, she raised her lips to be kissed. She was a handsome woman and her lips were thick and inviting, but the thought of kissing her disgusted him. Who was she, this phoney star? Who were any of these inauthentic people? If he could meet just one who wasn't obeying some outside force, someone able to recognise the capacity to choose and employ it. She pulled his head down to hers and pressed her lips against his mouth. He thought of M and their trysts and wished he could be with her. When she yanked him in the direction of her cabin he complained of feeling sick.

"Oh, don't fail me now, darling."

"I think it was the flight. I'd better go to my cabin."

"No, come to mine. I've got something to settle your stomach."

By feigning sickness he managed to prevent intimacy. When she was asleep, he crept out onto the deck. Maybe he should grab a lifejacket and jump after all. His minder appeared.

"Stomach feeling better?"

"Much."

"We're heading back to land. There's a bit of a crisis."

"What's that?"

"It happens now and again. Trouble with the outsiders. We quell it quickly."

"Nothing to do with me."

"Everything's to do with you now."

He returned to bed wondering how he would keep the super-star at bay in the morning, but anxious over what his minder had said. Trouble? Did that mean violence? Well, if they continued to look after him, at least he wouldn't be caught up in that. Yet something in the way she'd spoken, not her meaning but her tone, troubled him. He ran the words over in his head. It was as if she was implicating him. There was trouble and he had to know about it. It was his affair. He dreamt the celebrity was ripping off his clothes as they flew in an armed helicopter firing air-to-ground missiles, rockets, volleys of bullets as they skimmed the tops of the waves. As they crashed into the water he woke in a sweat. Trouble, what the hell did she mean?

He was up early. When the super-star roused, sober and somewhat queasy she took herself off to the bathroom and called to him from the shower. He refused to go to her, slipped out to the deck and watched for the appearance of land. Two fighter aircraft cracked the air above, climbing steeply as if gravity was an illusion.

"Impressive, aren't they?" said his minder.

"If you like that kind of thing."

"They're necessary."

"If you like killing people."

"It's not a matter of liking. It has to be done."

"That's always the excuse. Killing people is the hobby of the powerful."

"Where's your partner from last night?"

"Washing off her hangover."

"Had breakfast?"

"Not yet."

"Let's eat together."

"How long before we dock?"

"We're full speed."

"Is it war?"

"Let's not exaggerate. We'll see, but what has to be done, we'll do."

There was an obvious sense of urgency, but all the same his needs were attended to. He tried to restrain his appetite and eat a minimal breakfast, but the sumptuous array and the desire for more the more he ate drove him to eat to satiety. His minder tried to cajole him to play deck games, to float on the pool, to watch a film, but his nerves were attuned to the background sense of tension. When they docked a uniformed delegation, guarded by soldiers in fatigues carrying automatic weapons, boarded. Why were they here? There were a dozen hedonists on the boat. What use could they be in battle? His minder disappeared for a couple of hours as did the captain. She reappeared to lead him down the gangway and into her car which sped away along roads he didn't recognise.

"The military seem interested in you," he said.

"Marginally."

"Where are we going?"

"Everything has to be in state of readiness."

"What's that to do with me?"

"It has to do with everyone."

"I'll choose what is and isn't my business."

"Is staying alive your business?"

"Staying away from fighting is."

"That may not be possible."

Was he going to suborned into joining their war? What did it have to do with him? He wanted to protest angrily, but what good would it have done? Decisions were being made. The machine, probably. One decision after another had been made since he walked into the building for the interview, which still hadn't happened, except this was the interview, they said. If they made him wear a uniform, set him marching and obeying orders, maybe that would be the moment to fight back decisively. Yet what could he do against an entire people? How many were they? It might be a few hundred thousand or millions. The one thing he could do was to refuse. Non-cooperation might get him some kind of punishment, though what had happened so far was punishment. He'd been punished with luxury and service. It was a kind of mockery. If he shook his head at a uniform, dropped the gun, would they continue to treat him like a spoilt prince? He remembered the restaurant and the old man in the cottage. Perhaps he would be seized, bound, thrown in a cell and shot through the head like a rabid dog.

They arrived at what seemed some sort of camp in that it was composed of more or less identical buildings laid out symmetrically. At its entrance was a flag he'd never seen before atop a pole ten metres high: a sun rising behind a horizon between a broad red stripe on the inside edge and a gold one at the outer; beneath it a slogan in an alphabet he didn't recognise.

"What does that mean?"

"From the beginning of time."

"Really? That's about fourteen billion years ago, isn't it?"

"Depends who you believe."

Everything was very neat. The roads were punctuated with gentle speed bumps which kept their speed to ten. At a T-junction, a soldier saluted them.

"He knows you," said X.

"Maybe."

"Why does he have to salute you?"

"Because he's a soldier."

"Do you have rank?"

"In a way."

They pulled up outside what seemed to be the largest building, in the middle of the site. The flag was there again, on a pole jutting from the wall at an obtuse angle. Three white painted steps in a semi-circle led to the double, wooden doors whose panels where ten-centimetre squares of glass. Above, a stone canopy, painted in the same way and imitating the form of the steps offered shelter. At either side were large, bay windows which struck X as more domestic than official.

They were greeted by a young, female soldier who opened the door and saluted. She was petite and blonde, her hair curled behind her small ears, her eyes very blue in the light. X noticed her face was made-up: long, black eyelashes, red lipstick, toner applied to her skin. Her skirt was tight and ended above the knees and on her feet were black high heels. She gave him a coy smile, ducked her chin and batted her lids.

In the foyer were two long, blue velvet sofas. On both, women in uniform were reading magazines. They saluted perfunctorily. The minder led him along a corridor whose sides were glass and beyond, left and right, were gardens full of colour and lush growth. She knocked on a heavy wooden door marked with a name, he heard the call and they entered. Behind a wide, polished desk whose surface was clear sat a woman of thirty-five. Her black hair framed her pale face on which sat a charming, self-effacing half-smile. X noticed her dark eyes and her long fingers.

"Your new recruit," said the minder.

The woman stood up and reached her hand across the desk. X shook it and felt its softness.

"We'd better get you settled in," she said.

"As a matter of fact, I've no intention of staying."

The two women looked at one another.

"I must get going," said the minder.

"Just a minute," said X, but she was out of the door and the woman in uniform was by his side with her hand on his forearm. X was confused by his sense of attachment to the minder. He was almost impelled to run after her and beg to go with her; but why? He had no connection to her which mattered. As a matter of fact, he despised her. Yet he felt she'd delivered him to a second degree of alienation which made her almost as reassuring to him as his mother.

"Don't worry, we'll get you installed and looked after. You'll be fine."

She smiled in a girlish, modest way, as if they might have met at a party or in the pub. He followed her along more corridors from which the sumptuous gardens were visible till she opened a door and showed him into his suite, as plush as a five-star hotel.

"What do you think?"

"Fine."

"Anything you want just lift the receiver."

"Okay. But this is a military facility, isn't it?"

"Of course."

"Are there any men here?

"Only you."

He was silenced for a second.

"Then why am I here?"

"We'll look after you."

"I understood there was a crisis."

"There is, but it's not existential. We have these things to deal with now and again. We call it housekeeping."

"So I've been brought here because I might be involved."

"No, because you are involved. Make yourself at home. Someone will come for you when it's time to eat."

He was no more away from what he knew here than since the day of the putative interview, yet he couldn't quell the sense that in being separated from his minder he had lost something. He told himself he was a fool and should pull himself together, but the feeling wouldn't subside. In response, his ideas quickened to escape. No doubt security here was intense. What would they do if he simply walked off the camp? Shoot him? Drag him back? Maybe the women with the nice smile would cajole him, put her soft hand on his arm and speak sweetly to him. He would have to bide his time. If he was to be involved in training, he would get to know the lie of the land, have a weapon in his hands.

He lay on the bed trying to convince himself some obvious means of getting away would present itself but as the minutes passed his mood changed: since the day he walked through door to attend the interview, there had been no significant opportunity. The appalling thought occurred to him he would die here; but that was absurd. He was a young man. There were decades ahead. Already, a serious search for him would have been instigated at home.

A gentle knock interrupted his thoughts.

"Come in."

The blonde soldier entered. She'd taken off her tunic and unbuttoned her short-sleeve blouse. Setting herself on the side of the bed she asked him if he was ready to eat.

"I could manage something."

"I'll take you to the restaurant."

"Don't you call it a canteen or a mess or something."

"You'll eat with the officers. The food is very nice."

"Where are we?"

"A military camp."

"Yes, but have you heard of Y?" and he mentioned the name of his home town.

She shook her head.

"It's a nice place, in a way. I could take you there."

"I wouldn't be allowed."

"Well, break the rules."

"No one ever does that."

"How do you know?"

"Everyone knows."

"The machine watches you."

"Yes."

"How do you know the machine exists?"

"Without it we wouldn't know how to live."

They entered a dining-room where soldiers were seated at long tables arranged in rows. There was a hubbub of conversation, an atmosphere of camaraderie and pleasantness. Waiters, also in military uniform, were carrying circular trays balanced on the upturned fingers of one hand. The necks of wine bottles protruded from ice buckets. On each table burned three tall candles.

"You can sit on the end there."

"Am I the only man?"

"Yes."

"Why?"

"This is a female regiment."

"Then why am I here?"

"A decision must have been made."

He sat next to an upright woman with broad shoulders and a long, narrow face with a thin blade of a nose and opposite a smaller one, plump, wearing glasses whose narrow eyes creased into a smile. They made small-talk and were very friendly, as were the other women . He was served mushroom soup, cod, beef, roast potatoes, carrots, green beans, gravy, apple crumble and ice-cream, cheese and biscuits, coffee.

"You eat well here," he said.

"We do," said the plump women.

"An army marches on its stomach," he said.

They looked blank.

"I feel a bit odd," he said, "being the only man and the only one not in uniform."

"They'll get you kitted out tomorrow," said the plump one.

"Yes, I guess the fighting will start soon," he said.

Neither responded.

As they were drinking their coffee, an officer entered and they all stood to attention. For a second, he stayed seated, but awkwardness and fear forced him to his feet and made him pull himself upright. He felt vaguely foolish and was tempted to flop into his chair and say:

"Carry on. What has this dumb show to do with me?"

It reminded him of his uncle's funeral when his mother had been dabbing her eyes with a handkerchief and he was tempted to crack a joke. The inappropriateness of his feelings troubled him. Was he at fault or the occasion?

The officer had a cluster of medals on her chest. Her uniform was black while all the others were grey. She carried a highly polished stick, with a gold handle and ferrule. She commanded her troops to sit. X did so, feeling it was absurd he should obey her.

Many centuries ago, the officer began, when our forbears arrived in this land, they had to struggle to survive. It is thanks to their fortitude and bravery we live so well. As you know, we have no greater wish than to live at peace with our neighbours, but as you know also we have to be constantly aware of possible threats. Rare though they are they can unsettle us. We have never been in fatal danger since The

Great Victory. Our borders are secure. Our forces ever alert, well-armed and trained. I know you will have expected to carry out your service without having to put yourselves at risk. The crisis we face today is not of our making. We have exerted every effort to avoid conflict. I know you will all do your duty. I hope to see you here again once this episode is over, but to those of you who may not be present, reflect that your sacrifice will permit our civilisation to continue.

Everyone applauded. X joined in.

The blonde walked him back to his suite.

"So the fighting is imminent," he said.

"I don't know."

"That's what the officer was saying, wasn't it?"

"Maybe. We'll find out when we need to know."

He stopped.

"Some of you are going to die."

"We have to."

"Don't you have the right to know why?"

"We trust the decisions."

"Of a machine?"

"Wherever the decisions come from."

When they arrived she asked him coyly if there was anything else she could do for him. For a second he wondered if he should invite her in and try to persuade her to help him, but looking into her eyes he saw her willingness to do what she was instructed. He told her he was ready to sleep and that probably he was going to have a demanding day ahead. She agreed and left him.

During the night he was woken by the sound of vehicles. He looked out of his window but could see nothing. He slipped out with a towel round him and followed the corridors to the entrance where he saw armoured cars passing in convoy. A soldier appeared from the darkness.

"Can't you sleep?"

"No. I thought I heard something, you know, something unusual."

"Would you like me to help you get back to sleep?"

"No, no. I'll be fine."

His anxiety began to rise. In bed he was unable to settle. He would refuse a uniform. What was he doing in a women's regiment anyway? In any regiment? They couldn't force him. He wasn't going to take part in this madness, whatever it was. All of them heading into killing with no idea why. Some decision had been made somewhere by someone or something and they were willing to die because of it. He wasn't. It was time for confrontation. He wanted no more fancy meals, warm beds and obliging women. He was going. That was that. One way or another he'd find his way.

In the morning three soldiers came for him. They handed him his uniform, waited till he showered and shaved and helped him dress.

"Very smart," said one of them. "Look in the mirror."

He surveyed himself and was appalled.

"Don't you feel like a soldier?"

"Yes."

One marched in front and two at either side. They arrived at a parade ground where he was presented with an automatic weapon and put in line. They marched, turned, marched in the opposite direction, turned, stood to attention at the orders from a stocky, dark-haired woman. For hours they went through the same routine. His calves ached. He wanted to throw down the weapon and walk away. Why not? He wasn't part of this. How did he belong here? Yet he looked around him at the hundreds of women with weapons and feared what they might do. Who knew what instructions they'd been given?

At length they were marched off to a low building, less inviting than the rest, a functional changing room where they took off their smart uniforms, hung them in lockers and donned fatigues. The women removed their clothes without demur. He kept from looking at them and concealed himself as best he could. As he pulled on his boots which rose several centimetres above his ankles, one of the women said:

"Ready for thirty kilometres?"

"What?"

"I love it. You feel so full of energy the next day."

"Oh," and he tied his laces tight.

They had to heave hefty backpacks onto their shoulders before they set off. Quickly out of the camp, they climbed a hillock where X stumbled on the divets and lumps. At its summit they saw more hills, taller, disappearing in the distance where mist covered their peaks. They climbed and descended, crossed streams, bogs which grabbed at their feet and made their thighs ache, jogged along stony tracks, cut away into woods where the paths where hardly wide enough to accommodate them one at a time. X became impossibly thirsty and stopped to take the drink bottle from the pocket of his backpack.

"Keep running, soldier," an officer said and pushed him.

He reasoned they would pause soon. How far had they run? Maybe ten miles. There would have to be a break for food and drink or people would start to collapse in the heat. Yet they went on. If the pace slackened the officers chivvied them. A women fell to her knees. An officer grabbed her shoulders and yanked her upright.

"When do we get to eat?" said X when an officer passed him.

"When you prove you're worth it."

The first woman to get left behind vomited, fell to her knees and collapsed by the side of a path.

"Hey," shouted X. "She needs help."

"Look after yourself, soldier," said an officer. "Get running."

X saw five or six women fall and fail to get up. Were they going to be left to die out here?

They came to a climb whose prospect sapped his will. His legs were trembling. His mouth was so dry he could barely swallow. Maybe if he gave up and they left him to die he would be able to recover and make his escape, but when he fell to his knees, an officer grabbed his backpack and lifted him.

"You're nearly home, soldier. Don't let yourself down."

Let himself down? He had no desire to be here. This was none of his business. There was no question of letting himself down by not doing what was ordered from without. He struggled up the steep slope, fell, raised himself by grabbing at the rough grass. Nearly home. Food and drink. Sleep. His body no longer belonged to him. He saw himself climbing, as if his consciousness floated away from his physical self. Calm and observing, his sense of self saw him

163

as a pathetic, hopeless figure without autonomy. Yet he found some residual strength. Beyond the peak, the camp loomed into view. He tripped on the descent and rolled several hundred metres.

"Clumsy," said an officer. "To your feet."

Back in the changing room the women sat on the benches, lay on the floor. X collapsed in a corner without the energy to search for his water bottle. A few minutes to recover and he'd find it. An officer ordered them into the showers. The women began to strip and file through.

"You too, soldier."

"Give me a few minutes."

"You won't have a few minutes in battle," she said. "Get in the shower."

He began to unlace his boots with twitching fingers, pulled off the right one, stopped, found his bottle and drank. Swallowing was difficult. Small sips, he said to himself. Naked women were walking by to the showers. He averted his eyes. The water was tepid but still enormously relieving. He filled his mouth and held it. If he could stay here and drink, fall asleep, his heart might calm down, he might feel ready to get to his feet.

"You two," said an officer, "get him out of his uniform."

The pair of women, dripping with cold water, began to unfasten him, as if he was a baby.

"I can do it, I can do it."

They stood by and watched him. He was shy of his nakedness. Dozens of unclad women could see him. He shuffled to the shower where an officer in uniform stood at either end.

"This way."

The icy water made him judder and contort. He tried to rub himself to summon some warmth. From either end the officers watched him. There was soap in little chrome racks at the side of each spray.

"Get yourself clean," called one of the officers.

The cold produced hardly any lather. He did his best before trying to leave. The officer checked her watch.

"Two more minutes."

He went back under, his teeth chattering. His hands were turning blue. Most of the women had finished. He hugged himself but the chill penetrated. When his time was up one of the officer's called:

"Out now, soldier. Three minutes to get into your uniform."

Towels were being thrown to the women who rubbed themselves vigorously. X pulled his around his shoulders, tried to dry his face and hair. Three minutes. The women were used to the routine and moved quickly. Yes. If he removed the cold water as rapidly as he could and got into his clothes he would warm up. He took a swig from his bottle.

"No time for that. Get your uniform on."

The cold and tiredness prevented him working with energy. His sides were still damp, his feet were painfully cold. He was the last to be dressed. His vest was sticking to patches of damp. His socks were twisted. He was still shivering. They marched back to the dining-room which was now empty of tables. Rows of chairs faced a lectern. He'd hoped they were to be given hot food. He tried to sit on the back row but an officer guided him to the front. In spite of the warmth, he was still cold. His limbs felt thin and weak. His heart raced and he was light-headed.

An officer, not the one who addressed them previously, came to the lectern. Like the first, she was garlanded with medals but she was older, her hair was grey, the skin of her neck had begun to sag. She spoke slowly and in a thin voice.

You have all done well today. You have proved your fitness and readiness for battle. Your training has prepared you and you know you must do what you are ordered. The machine has processed all the available data and the war begins tomorrow. Have confidence that whatever you are told to do comes from the most exalted intelligence the earth has ever seen. Do not question. We can't move forward if we doubt. Progress is ours. The outsiders are planning an attack. We shall pre-empt them. Nothing you do can be wrong. Have absolute confidence. They are evil, backward people. We are the children of the machine. The world belongs to us. We shall flourish on it. Do your duty.

She strode away, stiff-backed to loud applause. At once the soldiers began to remove the chairs, the tables were reinstalled, laid with cloths and cutlery, they sat at their places and food was brought by soldier-waiters. X reached for a jug of water, filled his glass and emptied it in gulps. The soup steaming in front of him he devoured without looking up. He ate his main course so rapidly he began to feel queasy. His digestion seemed not to work, but he was feeling warmer. Sweat broke out on his forehead. He was struck by an irresistible desire to sleep. He lay his head on the table but an officer pulled him upright. The meal over they filed out and he was allowed to return to his suite where he flopped onto the bed in his uniform, pulled the duvet over him and closed his eyes.

His stomach and mind were troubled and the sleep he so craved wouldn't arrive. In the hinterland between sleep and wakefulness his mind swam with images. A vicious dog had him trapped; an old man held a shotgun to his head; a little girl brought him food; an endless line of naked women offered him sexual pleasure while he tried vainly to push them away or hide himself; he was speeding along in a car driven by a woman he didn't know; the roads and lanes seemed at one moment familiar, at the next, unknown; he ran up mountains carrying impossible burdens; freezing water cascaded on him; he entered a building to be interviewed, the receptionist took off her clothes and led him to a bathroom; he was climbing out of a window onto a roof which gave way beneath his feet; he was in the pub with M trying to explain what had happened to him; his mother was putting a plate of food in front of him; bombs began to fall close to him, he had a weapon and began to shoot indiscriminately.

When he woke, he realised he'd been asleep for several hours. His heart had calmed. He got to his feet and felt heaviness in his legs. His shoulders were aching. Back to him came the idea of imminent war. It was too insane. He had to find a way to escape. Yet he knew at once it was impossible. The light was beginning to diminish. What would happen? Would he be dragged from his bed early? He went into the bathroom and drank a glass of water. Looking in the mirror, he saw the face of what he used to be, before the interview. Determinedly he left the room, strode to the main building. An officer was crossing the entrance foyer.

"Excuse me," he said, "there's been a terrible mistake. I was supposed to have an interview…"

"That's been taken care of."

"No, no. I haven't been interviewed. The point is…"

"We know all we need to know. There's no need for any further questions."

"Yes, there is. From me. An interview works both ways. I want to withdraw."

"From what?"

"From the interview process."

"But you didn't apply."

"I know. I was invited and I turned up."

"How can you withdraw if you didn't apply?"

"Then I can leave?"

"Of course not."

"You can't keep me here against my will."

"It's not against your will. As you say, you turned up."

"I didn't accept anything."

"Then why did you come for the interview?"

"I needed a job."

"You've got a job."

"Have I?"

"You're a soldier. You've been well looked after. Haven't you?"

"Yes. In a way."

"Then what have you to complain about? Do what your job requires."

"I didn't accept this job. There was no process."

"You respond to an invitation because you want a job. You're housed, fed, your sexual appetites are satisfied.

You're part of a community. Now, don't be unreasonable. Do what you're told and all will be well."

She strode away. He swung open the main door and ran, unsure of which direction he should take. No one appeared. His legs didn't want to make the effort, but he forced himself. He was out of the camp and still no one was coming after him. If he could get far enough, if he could hide. If he could be absent when the fighting began. After a couple of kilometres, he slowed to walking pace. There was a path to his left between hedges and trees, he took it and climbed a steep tarmac path which at its mid-way point became suddenly more demanding. To his right was a metal rail about a metre high, he grabbed it and pulled himself along. He emerged between two houses, the one on the right with an extensive garden where an old woman was tending raspberry canes, the one on the left hidden behind high hedges. Two soldiers appeared, one at either side.

He slept hardly at all. At five in the morning the knock came, a head appeared and he was told to get up. While he was in the bathroom, his combat uniform arrived. He pulled it on and went to the dining-room. There was an air of great excitement, as if before a sporting contest, a party, a holiday. The soldiers were animated, talkative and in a high mood. He managed to sit next to the blonde.

"Everyone seems happy," he said.

"Yes, it's a great day."

"The start of war is a great day?"

"We can win the final victory."

"I thought you'd won that already. Have you been attacked?"

"We are always attacked."

"I mean militarily."

"The outsiders may attack any time."

"Wouldn't it be best to wait?"

"Why? We know they want to attack us."

"Why attack first?"

"We have to defend ourselves."

"But you haven't been attacked."

"We might be. Anyway, you're one of us."

"Wouldn't it be sensible to go to war only as a last resort?"

"It is a last resort."

"How can it be, if there has been no attack."

"An attack could come any time."

"It is coming, from you."

"From us."

She gave him a hard look.

"Have you been in battle before?"

"Several times."

"Killed people?"

"Lots."

She nodded and pressed her lips together as she looked at him, complaisant to her own accomplishment.

"This time they might get you."

"Doubt it. But we have to fight. They are brutes."

Who were brutes? The outsiders, whoever they were. He was one., at least he assumed. Except now they made him one of them, regardless of his origin or wishes. Here he was in unform, about to fight against himself.

"I'm not going to fight," he said.

"You've been ordered."

"By the machine."

"Probably."

"Why am I in a female regiment?"

"Because a decision was made."

"A mad decision. I should be with the men."

"There must be some reason. The decisions are always the best."

"It's obviously a mistake."

"The machine doesn't make mistakes."

"How do you know?"

"We know. Look how we live. That's because of the right decisions."

"Maybe it's because you attack people before they attack you."

"We attack only those who might attack us."

"I'm not going to fight."

"You will, when they're shooting at you."

He was struck by sudden anxiety. Into his head came the idea of himself as a child, playing soldiers with his friends, running through the garden with a plastic rifle in his hands, hiding in the garage, playing dead on the front lawn. Was he really going to be facing bullets, bombs, shells? Was some intent sniper going to fix him in his sights, pull the trigger and release several dozen rounds? A thousand bullets to kill a man, they say. But what was any of this to do with him? Decisions had been made. How could he be expected to kill or be killed without making the decision himself?

She was calmly sipping her coffee, as if she would be spending the day in front of a screen or answering telephones or teaching children the alphabet. The room was full of young women, brimming with life, about to enter the field of death. Decisions had been made. They began to leave their seats and head for the doors. Perhaps he should simply stay there, refuse to move, wait for them to lift him from his chair like a sit-down protester being carried off by the police.

"We need to get ready," she said.

"I'm staying here."

"Don't. If you refuse, they'll put you on the front line without a weapon."

He turned to her and she smiled, put her delicate hand on his shoulder.

"Come on. You'll be on the winning side. We'll wipe them out this time."

He left with her. She held his hand as they followed the path between the neat lawns.

"Would you like me to come to your room?"

"What for?" he said.

"I'll be nice to you, before we go into battle."

"Don't frustrated men make better soldiers?"

She kissed him on the lips and turned away.

"See you in a minute. The helicopters will be here soon."

An officer came to his suite and inspected him. He had an overwhelming desire to shoot her. The automatic was in his hands, like the plastic gun in the garden. He could pull the trigger and put an end to this farce. Yes, they would kill him, but he might well be killed anyway. Terror was in his viscera. He would be incapable of killing the supposed enemy. Who were they? They might be people he knew. Or absolute strangers. He had no motivation to kill.

"Good," said the officer. "On your way, the helicopters are landing."

The tandem-rotor machines were the same colour as the regimental uniform. They descended slowly and touched down with balletic grace. The soldiers climbed into their chunky fuselages, their loads on their backs. They might have been embarking on a pleasure trip. He stood aside, as if the whole episode might pass, the craft might take off and leave him behind, but an officer took him by the arm and directed him. He climbed the steps and crouched in the interior with a dozen women.

"Excited?" said his neighbour.

"Sure."

The rotors were turning. The noise of the engine was overwhelming. He wanted to get to his feet and shout:

"This is all a huge mistake. I came for an interview. I'm not a soldier. I'm not one of you. I'm an outsider."

The ladder was pulled up, the door slammed fatally shut. He was overcome by claustrophobia. Once in the air, they would be a target. How far was the enemy? They might be shot down before they got anywhere. This ludicrous metal crow might be his coffin. How stupid, to defy gravity for the purpose of being blasted to shreds by someone you've never met. A terrible sense of fatalism came over him which he valiantly tried to combat. Once out of this machine, he might be able to skedaddle. Wasn't war chaos? He could play dead, like on the front lawn. They'd leave him. When quiet reigned, he could slip away.

He hadn't expected the parachute. The door was opened, the sense of being buffeted, at the mercy of the wind , was exhilarating and frightening. The first trooper's static line was attached, she was counted down and jumped. The second, the third. No doubt they'd done it before. They knew how to manipulate the parachute, how to land. At what speed would he hit the ground? The officer gave him the nod. He stood up feeling his legs quake and his bowels melt. The line was clipped. Three. Two. One. He kept his eyes closed till deployment.

He could see the others below and around. What kind of territory was he to land in? He was scanning for signs of combat. What if was to be shot at as he fell? Here he was, a floating target. Hey, have a pot shot at me ! A giddiness arose in him. He wanted to make a joke of it all, like at the funeral.. Was he going to die before he hit the ground, be wounded or would he break his ankles and lie in hopeless pain until the enemy arrived and blew out his brains. Who with any brains would be here? The interview. Why had he gone? Out of some conviction that any blandishment from without must be in his interest, that the people inviting were on his side?

The ground came up at him swiftly. He clung to the risers tried to run as his feet connected but tripped and ended wrapped in nylon. He'd been told how to extricate himself but it didn't come quickly to mind. He struggled to pull himself to his feet.

"Quick release buttons, soldier," a voice said.

Three rings, he recalled, pulled the cord and was able to wriggle free. Around him, soldiers were running with their automatics deployed. He heard the roar of engines. Bulldozers were moving in from behind. A hundred metres ahead was a tall, wire fence interspersed with observation posts. Overhead began the buzzing of drones. He was standing watching. Alongside the bulldozers were armoured cars packed with troops.

"Move, soldier."

He began to walk forward. A drone took out an observation post. There was no defensive fire. Beyond the fence he could see people running. Were they soldiers? He couldn't discern any weapons. He spotted a child, looked for an officer.

"Hey," he called to whoever might hear, "there's a kid behind that fence."

Soldiers gestured to him to keep moving forward. He realised there were no men among them. Were men driving the bulldozers or operating the drones? Women with cutters were opening up the fence, peeling back great sections and rushing through. He saw them firing, witnessed a couple of bodies hitting the ground. Were they soldiers? The bulldozers were gaining on him. He stood aside and watched them plough past. No, they were driven by women. More drones flew by. Helicopters appeared, chugged beyond the fence and began to shoot. Grenades, rockets, machine-gun fire. Some small building exploded and was wrapped in flame? What was that? A house? Surely not. Some military installation? Still he could see no sign of soldiers nor of enemy fire. He went on slowly. His fellow soldiers were haring onwards as to face a fierce foe. Plainly now he saw a woman with a child in her arms fleeing the fence. She fell forward.

"Stop!" he shouted. "That was a woman and her kid. What the .."

An officer grabbed him by the shoulder and yanked him forward. He resisted, twisted out of her grasp.

"Do your duty, soldier."

"They're civilians."

"We do what we're told."

"No one's shooting at us. This is murder."

"Get moving. Now."

He trotted a little out of fear she would shoot him. When he felt safe, he stopped. The bulldozers reached the fence which fell like a house of cards before a strong breath. The soldiers rushed through, the helicopters danced above, their rockets screeching into the little buildings which more and more seemed to be places where people lived. The blonde was beside him. He grabbed her.

"What is this?"

"It's a great victory."

"But there are no soldiers."

"No, we planned it well."

"You're killing civilians."

"They're the enemy."

"But they're unarmed. Take them prisoner. You can't kill unarmed civilians. And there are kids."

"That's how they behave, they hide behind them."

He took hold of her weapon. She tugged and tussled.

"Let go! Let go or I'll shoot," she said.

He released his grip. She trained the rifle on him.

"Now move. Quick. They're getting away."

He turned his back on her and walked slowly but she prodded him with the barrel so he had to skip and increase his pace. As they drew closer he could discern the buildings were little, makeshift, wooden houses. A helicopter dipped its nose, fired a quick succession and one of them was thrown in the air, shattered planks falling as fire raged.

"There might have been people in there," he said.

"Good," she said.

An old man came hobbling through the fence, his hands in the air. He was thin and bent and walked stiffly, as if his knees no longer worked. He was waving his hands from side to side. On his face was a look of fear, desperation and incomprehension. X took a step towards him.

"Shoot him," she said.

"He's a harmless old man."

"He may be booby trapped. Shoot him."

"You're crazy," said X. "You people have gone crazy. It's okay," he called to the man. "I won't hurt you."

A volley of bullets hit the codger in the chest. He was blown backwards, fell limp and awkward, his aged blood spread slowly. X stood and looked at him. He turned to the blonde but said nothing.

"Take no chances," she said. "He can't hurt us now."

"The only good outsider is a dead outsider?"

"Yes."

He shook his head and walked away from the fence, back in the direction he'd come but she barred his way.

"I'm not part of this."

"Oh, you are."

"Shoot me if you like, but I'm going no further."

"Drop your gun."

He threw it to the ground. She summoned two soldiers who took him by the arms and marched him beyond the fence. A girl of twelve or so ran from one of the houses, a soldier came after her and shot her in the back. A bulldozer crashed into a side wall, the roof began to cave in, a mother emerged, three small children by her legs. Instantly all four of them were shot. Before them was a pile of half a dozen charred bodies. Dozens of men and women of all ages, teenagers, toddlers were trying to flee. Beyond the houses which formed a little, linear community was an open expanse, and in the far distance, the silhouettes of more, bigger, more concentrated buildings. As the villagers dispersed into this space, the soldiers pursued them, shot and cheered as they fell; the helicopters went after and strafed them, grenades exploded around them.

X's gun was thrust back into his arms.

"Run. Run and do your duty," the blonde said to him.

He turned to her, pulled the trigger and saw her head shatter. At once he was hit by a hundred bullets and fell forward as his warm blood was absorbed by the dry ground.

Three weeks later ,in the evening, the dining-hall was prepared. The long tables were set out, draped with starched white cloths. Each place setting had an equally beautifully laundered serviette held by a smooth wooden ring, a champagne flute, and a Bordeaux glass. The soldiers, washed, coiffuered and dressed in fresh, pressed uniforms took their places with smiles, hugs and pleasant greetings. A quartet composed of a pianist, a percussionist, a double-bass and a clarinettist played easy, recognisable melodies. Each table bore a candelabra with four branches. The lights were turned low. The officers were seated apart. Waitresses in white blouses, black skirts and aprons set bottles of sparkling water on each table, filled the flutes, put a bottle of red for each three diners. The white bean soup, tinged with lemon and green chillies, was served in shallow bowls with a gold rim. Each side plate had a thick slice of warm sourdough. The women chatted as they ate, raising a gentle hum, the atmosphere sedate and civilised. Attentive to their needs, the waitresses filled every empty glass, enquired if everything was to taste. The musicians played pianissimo, providing a charming background. Once the bowls had been efficiently removed, the side plates cleared, cured salmon with prawns and pickled salad with a dill and lime crème fraiche left the women wondering what they were about to taste. The speculation gave way to delight. They spoke of the diligence of the chefs, of the length of time they must have been at work, exchanged superlatives. Some wished they could request second helpings. The flutes were raised, sips of the sparkling used to clear the palate. Unexpectedly, a salade aux lardons appeared with peas, mushrooms, slices of beets, carrots, onions, basil, chives, flat leaf parsley. Some began to express satiety, yet relished the idea of the main course. The officers got to their feet, wandered, stopped to share a few words, smiled, touched a soldier or two on the shoulder. Roast grouse with creamed root vegetables, stuffed cabbage and elderberries sat, too sweetly arranged to be disturbed, before them. The clicking of the cutlery against the plates was the background percussion to their conversation. They ate slowly and with relish, the starters having taken the violent edge from their appetites. The pleasure of eating was accompanied by the memory of recent events, the total victory over their enemy, the annihilation of the threat to their well-being. The alcohol

179

softened their mood, made them garrulous and sociable. Old resentments were dissolved, bitter enmities evaporated.

Four desserts were set down once the empty plates had been removed: rich chocolate cake with a neat dollop of cream; pandoro tiramisu; plum berry spiced granola crumble with labneh; sticky date pudding with brown butter sauce. Spoilt for choice, some of them asked if they could have a portion of more than one. Most found a space for seconds. The chocolate cakes disappeared. Before the silver coffee pots and the charming, little, white cups and saucers came the cheeseboards. At their centre was a round of brie cut into sixteen wedges; black olives to the left, green olives to the right; Parma ham at twelve o'clock and six; interspersed, triangular slices or cubes of pecorino, Gruyère, asiago, edam, aged cheddar; packed closely, crackers, bread sticks, crostini and sliced baguette. They laughed at the idea of eating more, but one cracker topped with brie was enough to rekindle appetite and soon became two, three, a dozen.

The coffee was poured, the fat bellied pots of cream, lifted, the thick liquid poured over inverted spoons. A lectern was placed at the head of the tables. An officer entered from the doors at the opposite end and walked gracefully between the table as the soldiers applauded. She installed herself behind the lectern, the chatter subsided.

Ladies, I hope you have enjoyed your victory meal. It is my honour and pleasure to be with you on this splendid occasion. You have served your country well. There is no greater commitment than that we owe to our country. All else fades into meaninglessness. You have risen to the greatest height a human being can achieve by doing your duty on the battlefield. As you know, there have been times when we have fought valiantly without securing our aim. Indeed, we have faced the real possibility of defeat. Gladly, we have found the way to prevail. That we should is beyond question. There have been doubters. There have been those who have spoken of compromise. Compromise is another word for surrender. We will never compromise. We have renewed and advanced our military capabilities to the best available. We need fear no one, but many should fear us. We are people of peace. We wish nothing more than to live without conflict, but those who don't share our aims are an ever-present threat. Our rights go back to the beginning of time. There can be no question. The machine has told us so. How can we enjoy our rights when there are others who do not accept them? Can we cede to backward peoples? Can we grant they are our equals? That would be a betrayal of our history, of our extraordinary sacrifices. There is one clear trajectory and it is ours. How fortunate we are to have joined the stream of progress. We have been picked out. Never forget you belong to a special people. You have been called upon to fulfil an extraordinary destiny. Over the past three weeks you have shown yourselves up to the task. There are those who criticise us, of course. There always were and there always will be; but the more criticism we receive, the more we know we are right. They are our enemies because we are ahead of them, because we have been chosen. They will always claim we are violent, but we hate violence. Doesn't the machine tell us we are the most peaceable people ever? They will always claim we are prejudiced but we reject all prejudice. We have to annihilate them because they want to annihilate us. Yes, we attacked them. Of course, who will not attack an enemy planning to wipe them out? The machine tells us they want to wipe us out. We have fed all our data into the machine.

At this there was long applause which permitted her to pause and take a few sips of water.

You have carried out a great accomplishment. To annihilate an entire people in three weeks is a feat unprecedented in history.

There was more enthusiastic applause which she calmed by raising her palms.

Not a single one of our enemy remains alive to threaten us. All the children are dead, dispatched humanely, swiftly. From this neighbour, our most potent enemy, we face no threat. Their cities are rubble where rats scavenge. So they shall stay as a monument to their evil and our virtue. Their so-called places of learning are no more, their specious culture has been erased. That is a fine cleansing. Let the rain, the snow, the ice, the wind , the sun, wear away what once they dared call a civilization. Time will bury it all deep in the earth. Their existence, a scar on the planet, will be nothing but a thin layer in the deposits. So we can celebrate. We are safe. Till the next threat. We will never rest until all opposition to our doctrine is expunged. How can we when we know our doctrine is the truth? You have a period of respite. You can go back to your families, enjoy yourselves. For a short time you can relax. The benefits of our system are available. You have fought to defend them. You have undertaken the unpleasant task of slaughter, but eliminating a diseased people becomes a relief, like putting to death an animal struck by a terminal disease. Take your leave as a due reward. Go to the beaches, the mountains, the forests, the cities. Walk, ride, ski, swim, eat, love, and all the while congratulate yourselves. Centuries hence, people will look back on these last few weeks and marvel. You are heroines. No one can ever take that away from you. Tonight, you will take away your medals, but it is the medals within that matter. Nothing can sully the pride you rightly feel. You have rid the world of a plague, a blight. You have made our land safe for future generations. But the next threat is not far away. Has there ever been a time we weren't threatened? Take heart. Don't be anxious. We can't be beaten. You know where the next threat is coming from. They have long harboured the desire to annihilate us, which is why we must annihilate them. Those who say we should sue for peace, who want agreements, pacts, treaties, are cowards and backsliders. There can be no pacts with vicious, backward peoples. They are savages who understand only violence. We are the peace lovers, but there can be no peace till we triumph over evil. It is now my enormous pleasure to award you your medals, signs of the victory you won without the loss of a single life on our side. Long live our land. Long live the children of the machine.

*